Toujours vers toi, Richie

With gratitude to the South Bay Writers Workshop members who gave wise counsel and great critiques.

To the 11 people that not only read the column, but signed on as "Followers" which is an unfortunate word choice, I think, but you did it and God bless you.

Special thanks to Jay Simpson for imaginative and professional art direction.

Henry Greenleaf, age 10 at the time, for a creative consult about chapter headings.

"If you make someone laugh, you give them a little vacation." Winston Church

Other Authors Who Liked It

Girrrlll we could have had us some giggles! Oscar Wilde 1854-1900

Kin we tawk? Joan Rivers 1933-2014

You're too nice! You've got to let the rabid, feral *you* out! Rodney Dangerfield 1921-2004

My writers want a copy of this; can I get a discount? Bob Hope 1903-2003

Chapter 1 – Has Humor Changed?

Jokes have certainly changed because our times have changed. Example: illustration of a row of emoticons. Below that, another row of … hieroglyphics and the caption is: " 4,000 years and we're still using symbols to write."

Not exactly a thigh-slapper, was it? But who today under the age of 50, let's say, gets the concept of something being so funny that one slaps one's thigh in appreciation? Not enough to fill a stadium, that's for sure.

Richie, my husband has been excavating in the "store room" (not a joke, but it should be.) Periodically he brings me little treasures he's found. The most recent is a book "A Treasure of Laughter" written back in the late '20s and early '30s. Note this – people spoke politely back in the day and there are *no* vulgarities in the entire book. You have to take my word for this. Okay …

Two men, just released from the lunatic asylum meet on the street.

"First man: "Bet you can't guess what I've got in my hand."

Second man: "A battleship?"

First man looks in his closed hand a minute and says, "Nope."

"An automobile?"

Looks again. "No, try once more."

Second man shouts: "A horse!"

"Darn it! But, wait – what color?"

Second man says, "Green."

First man: "Ah hah! You peeked!"

***

Two morons had remarkably good luck on a fishing expedition. Toward the end of the day, one of them said, "This is a good spot. I wish we had some way of finding it tomorrow."

"Why don't you put a mark on the boat?" the other said.

"That sounds reasonable, but how do you know we'll get the same boat?"

* * *

Two good friends, Father Kelly and Rabbi Levy sat opposite each other at a banquet where a ham was being served. Father Kelly helps himself with gusto and turns to his friend and says, "When are you going to be liberal enough to eat ham?" The Rabbi says, "At your wedding."

A Virginian was boasting about his lineage and said, "One of my ancestors signed the Declaration of Independence."

The Jew looked down at the ground and said, "One of mine signed the 10 Commandments."

Chapter 2 - Turkeys, The Old New and the New New

Why Turkey?

Blame it on the Pilgrims. Turkey became the national bird of choice almost by default. Let us go back in time …

The Pilgrims were by no means well-to-do. They wanted a celebration, but they didn't want it to be so lavish that they had to eat corn cobs all winter. Worriedly, they cast their eyes around their barnyards for a suitable meat. (Vegetarianism was unknown at this point.)

Cows were immediately out of the running because they were much more useful alive than on the dinner table.

Roosters are famously tough eating and prep time did little to, er, soften them up.

Hens laid eggs and were productive on very little food.

Venison was too time-consuming – first, find a deer (plentiful it must be said – the NRA hadn't been invented yet either) and kill it, peel or skin it. The hides were useful, but the few wives who were fashionistas, were tired of "Always buckskin? Can't you find some minks?"

There were tons of hams and pork products, but they weren't considered chic enough for a holiday meal. (clearly they'd changed their minds by the time Easter rolled around.)

Turkeys won by default. They spent the first seven months of their doomed lives eating the insects and worms that plagued the farmer and by the time that

T-Day rolled around, they were usually a convenient size for the oven and then dinner.

Another factor that may have contributed to their demise was Charles Dickens. His book "A Christmas Carol" was published in 1843 and much was made of Scrooge's gift to the Cratchit family of a big, fat turkey. As the book was widely read in American, one thing led to another...

EVERYTHING OLD IS NEW AGAIN?

Can the trendies only find things that existed long, long ago? Is copying the only thing they're good for?

I'm referring to a new phrase in our American lexicon and that word is "shaming," as in "fat shaming" (and subsequent law suits.) How do you "shame' a morbidly obese person anyhow? Every time you spot one, start singing, "Fatty, fatty, two by four, couldn't get through the kitchen door!"?

Pointing out the obvious hardly seems "shaming." Presumably they buy their own clothing (size 22) and have seen themselves in mirrors? However briefly.

What muses me is that public shaming has existed since medieval days when a person who was caught red-handed at a minor sin was punished by being put in stocks in the village square or market entrance for predetermined length of time. The villagers were free to stand in front of the prisoner and lecture and/or jeer as much as they wanted. And if you've seen drawings of stocks, you know that the person was firmly there until released. Once put in them, they weren't going anywhere.

The next use of "shaming" was in the late '20s when English writers Alec Waugh and Nancy Mitford used it for a lot of misdeeds – "Dahling, she forgot to tip the waiter and he chased her out into the street!" (reply) "Dahling, how too shame-making!"

Today the insulters have taken to online media. This is hardly effective and not nearly as much fun as (presumably) standing in front of some malcontent, looking them straight in the eye and castigating them at length.

All I can snort is, "New, huh? I don't think so."

A NEW WORD FOR US

Verb: doxing, past tense: doxed, as in (said with some glee) "I doxed him!" This sounded rather sinister to me albeit at least bloodless. As opposed to "I offed him" for example. The Sopranos taught me all I want to know about that! Speaking of whom, the bathtub beheading did it for me; I never believed for one minute in the validity of that show after that.

Dox means document tracing. An opponent finds you despite your having a stage name, so to speak, online.

Example: you sign yourself as "Squeaky Wheel" and, thinking you are perfectly anonymous, write extremely rude comments online. If you have then offended another commentator sufficiently, they may be inspired enough to find out who you really are as in legal name, address, city, country. And then they tell the entire online world.

DO YOU KNOW YOUR SELL-BY DATE?

This heading was chosen rather than "Predicted Age at Time of Death" as it was thought to be more tactful. (tsk tsk) Some people get so jumpy about Death.

Incidentally, please note and believe that this is the most UN-scientific test possible and does not consider any factors aside from the ages of parents and grandparents at their time of death. Not what they died of nor what caused death.

If any of the above are still alive and flourishing, don't bother to take this test. You're too young to be considering things like your own demise. But just to be safe don't drink or text and drive, okay?

Begin this exam by writing down the ages of your parents when they died. We'll use my family as an example. They would want me to be helpful.

My father was 81; my mother was 87. Added together the sum is 168. Now divide 168 by two and we get 84 which is the age I can expect to pop my clogs. As I am now 75, nine years left seems a bit scant somehow.

My father's parents: his father died age 64, bringing the average 'way down, but his mother helped the cause by living to be 101 and five months.

My mother's parents: her mother died at 87, her father at 96.

516 is is the combined age of all of the above. Divide by six because there are six of them. The grand total is 86 which is better than 84!

Disclaimer: The above is presented to readers for amusement purposes and is not in any way to be considered seriously. This is just rainy afternoon fun.

Chapter 3 – Threatening Children, The First Ladies; a Comic Looks at Food

Global Threats

Writer Bill Bryson wrote of an encounter with an English shopkeeper whose demeanor was surly indeed. Leaving his establishment, Bryson muttered to himself, "Cheerless prick" which I thought was grand! When was the last time you heard "cheerless"? It seems to be used more often to describe weather – 'A cheerless, dark afternoon typical of a New York winter" is an example.

In fact, I often think the Brits have an edge on us Yanks when it comes to the appropriate descriptive phrases. Which thought naturally sent me scurrying around mentally (don't worry, short trip; didn't knacker me.)

Situation: You are babysitting for dear friends. The kids range in age from 4 to 11. I think you can leave them home alone by the time they're 12. They know where everything is. You know, TV/VCR, kitchen … and where you hid that box of chocolates.

Problem: these kids are misbehaving with what can only be described as vigor. What to do, what to do?

Obviously, you can't give them a fast wallop across the butt, as appealing as that may be. Parents react so hysterically when someone else administers corporal punishment.

This has worked for me in the past. Give the kid a stern look, slitting your eyes for added impact, regard them sternly and say, "If you don't stop that, I am going to do something so terrible to you that all of your grandchildren will be born with snow white hair!"

This is so vague – yet menacing somehow- that the kid will often stop the action to puzzle out what this could possibly be. At which point, you say, "Let's all sit down and have a cookie."

A Very Good Read

"First Ladies – An Intimate Group Portrait of White House Wives" by Margaret Truman Fawcett Books   335 pages $14.95 paperback

Few could be more qualified to write about these women. She is the only child of Bess and Harry Truman and, starting with Eleanor Roosevelt, she has known every living First Lady since 2008 when she died, age 83..

Rather than a dreary chronicle year by year, of what they were like, she has sorted them into classifications. To name a few of the 25 chapters...

"Pioneer Crusaders" Lucy (Lemonade Lucy) Hayes, the first presidential wife to have a college degree and the first to ban serving alcoholic beverages in the White House. (Entrepreneurs would pay staff for a "real" drink behind her back.)

"The Lost Companion" Eleanor Roosevelt. FDR cheated on her; she found the love letters from Another Woman and flatly refused ever to have anything to do with him at all. Let's say it was no accident that she spent most of the White House Years on the road.

"The First Lady Who Wanted the Job" Helen Taft who was more ambitious than her husband by far.

"Maternally Yours" Edith Roosevelt who brought all six children (including teen age Alice, daughter of his late first wife) to the White House where they terrorized the help and were not above scaring visitors. Barbara Bush arrived with five adult children and 10 grandchildren.

"The Glamor Girls" President Tyler's second wife Julia Gardener Tyler, Dolley Madison, Frances Folsom Cleveland.

I Like the Way He Thinks

"Food – A Love Story" by Jim Gaffigan
Crown Archtype   340 pages $26

Gaffigan works and earns a living as a stand-up comic (We will explore the sad dearth of lay-down comics in another column) to support a wife and their five children.

He likes to eat. In fact, he self-describes as an "eatie" not a "foodie," foodies being those who fly great distances to eat at the newest rave chef's place. I'm thinking of the one in Norway (?) that hand-gathers moss to serve with his reindeer meat concoctions.

This is a perfect bathroom book with short chapters that rove hither and thither. The geography of American food – Seabugland (East Coast lobsters, clams, oysters which he describes as a rock with snot on it;) eating Mexicoland and so forth.

He is not a fan of vegetables and describes kale as "bitter spinach with hair."

Sushi? A Japanese chef didn't pay his electric bill.

He describes prosciutto as for people who like to floss while eating meat.

Food trucks motto – Poison and Run!

For restaurant fun, he suggests calling your female server "Food Bitch." I gotta try this but only in places where we know the help. Soft start, "You ever been called a 'food bitch'?"

Chapter 4 – Gender Identification; Is You Is or Is You Ain't?

Goodbye, Purple Prince

The artist formerly known as some kind of invented symbol was found dead in an elevator in his industrial-like looking home.

The ensuing foo-fa-rah has been unbelievable to me who rarely gave him any thought at all after his initial splash.

Not because I didn't like him or his music, but because I couldn't figure out what the hell he/it was. I knew that he was tiny (5 ft. 2 in.;) wore lots of eye make-up and high heels. This last was understandable given his height. But the sequins? He looked vaguely Spanish to me, but it turns out that he identified as black.

He loved the ladies and his list of conquests was considerable. "Toy boy?" He was a devout Jehovah's Witness who didn't drink alcohol but the last photo of him alive was taken of him exiting a pharmacy.

Whoever you were, Rest in Peace.

Gender Nonsense

The recent furor about public bathrooms among every sex – male, female, gay, straight, transgender has gotten way out of hand. Example: a kindergarten sent out questionnaires for incoming 4 year olds, asking parents with which sex their 4 year old identified.

Here are statistics that I carefully gleaned from Social Security figures, based on name changes from one sex to another due to the necessity of having matching documents for such things as passports and other legal documents.

There are estimated 135,367 transgender persons. Of them, 65 per cent identified as male and 35 per cent as women. The entire US population is 318.9 million. The tail wags the dog?

Caitlin Jenner and Mickey Jean

The Jenner Story is finally being used to wrap fish. For far too long we were subjected to squealing in corners about "his bravery." (snort)

In contrast, more than 25 years ago at LAX this was taking place. Richie worked for a Major American Airline (MAA) and in those days, well before 911, employees and their spouses were allowed to park in Employee Parking and grab one of the trams at the various locations and ride in to the bowels of LAX to catch their flights.

The "trams" were actually shuttle buses. One of the drivers was named Mickey Jean who was formerly a man.

She was no better looking as a lady as she'd been as a gent, a point that seems to have been totally ignored by Caitlin Jenner, presented as she was on Vanity Fair. She tried to look like a 26 year old glamour puss at the rather ripe age of 65. But the hands never lie. Take a look at hers.

Mickey Jean remained age appropriate in dress and make-up. I never heard a word against her either. The general attitude seemed to be honest curiosity as to why any male would ever want to be a woman?

Mickey Jean never addressed these comments as none were ever made to her. She continued on her gruff way, black work shoes thumping briskly up and down the stairs of her tram as she went to and from her job, driving the tram.

Many years later, after her retirement, the ground crew was augmented by a young man who was clearly in to change because his announced change was quite clearly visible through his uniform shirt (probably a 36C) tucked into navy pants over black work shoes. I often wondered what passengers thought as they boarded and got a brief glimpse of he/she through a window as they stowed their bags.

The only comment even remotely detrimental that I ever heard was "She male" in reference to her and even that was always said with honest bewilderment by the ground crews.

So – Bruce to Caitlin was pretty much an ode to narcissism which had nothing to do with bravery. But the MAA employees working during transition, very much in the public eye? That's bravery to me.

MAA's Employment Retirement Club once had Bruce (as he most certainly was then) Jenner as the guest speaker at one of their monthly meetings. It was held somewhere in the '90s and he was still bragging about his 1976 Olympic gold. His talk was billed as an "inspirational story" but how much braver would it have been for him to casually hike up a bra strap during his lecture? His audience probably wouldn't even have blinked. They knew Mickey Jean and the She male.

Chapter 5 – Pizza With Your Pot; Which Wine with a Big Mac?

Pressing questions indeed. Let us seek knowledge...

California has long been billed as the land of flakes, fruits and nuts, perhaps the particular zaniness that takes place here has been forgotten or overlooked by residents outside of our fair, but misguided state. In the gentle spirit of friendly competition, betcha you don't have this! (So, hah!)

We can get medicinal marijuana deliveries to the house. (We used to get non-medicinal down on a certain corner. Or so I was told; I don't smoke dope.)

Speed Weed is said to circumvent Proposition D that regulates dispensaries. Meanwhile, a Seattle-based firm – Leafly – is moving into Speed Weed's territory with billboards promising not only a timely delivery, but as well with information on the various brands they carry.

Clearly, calling for a pizza is now completely eclipsed in coolness. A marketing genius for a pizza place should be on this. "First Speed Weed, then call us for a pizza! 10% Discount for Speed Weed customers!"

The Wine List for Fast Food

National Public Radio's Joshua Wesson is a wine advisor for "The Splendid Table." He was interviewed about which wines with fast foods? And before you get all giddy, a stern reminder that having an open container (of alcohol) in your vehicle is a one-way ticket to jail.

Big Mac – the sauce is a nice combination of sweet and tart so go for a slightly sweet or off-dry Gewurtztrammer or Chenin Blanc.

Taco Bell Spicy Burritos – there's a reason most people drink beer with Mexican foods so look for a sparkling wine – not champagne, but perhaps prosecco.

Twinkies – with that cloyingly sweet, gloppy center, you need a palate cleanser – Asti Spumante!

Incidentally, O/T, if you will, but not really … Cheryl Forberg, writing for Spy magazine says that champagne is good for you.

Flutes only hold 4 to 6 ounces; only 90 to 135 calories (versus 5,000 for egg nog or 750 for a margarita.) The bubbles may force you to sip, not slug it down which is another portion control. Champagne is high in antioxidants "that may boost your brain power." She says "may," but I say, "Damned straight!"

Chapter 6 – Country Sayings and Boxer Trash Talking

"Butter My Butt and Call Me a Biscuit by Allen Zudo and Gene Cheek   198 pages $6.75

Should you desire to major in "country" here are some lines from the above book. There are longer pieces in it, but these are easier to remember as they are one-liners.

My piggy bank is as useful as an ashtray on a motorcycle.

We can't all be big shots. Someone has to sit on the curb and wave at 'em as they go by.

He's so rich, he buys a new boat every time his old one gets wet.

Money thinks I'm dead. (Many of us can relate ...)

He's so lucky, he could sit on a fence and the birds would feed him.

If times get any better, I'll have to hire somebody to help me enjoy them. (Ed. Note – Attention young blonde homewreckers)

One day you're drinking wine; the next you're picking grapes.

One day you're the peacock, the next day you're the feather duster.

I'm so poor I had to fry up my nest egg.

The new broom might sweep clean, but the old broom knows the corners.

He's been chased through the forest of mean and hit every tree trunk. (First cousin to: I been in sorrow's kitchen and licked out every pot.)

I'd have to get better just to die.

Who licked all of the red off of your candy?

Fine dining invitation: Let's go get greasy 'round the mouth.

A woman is wearing a tight-fitting, low-cut mini dress and a man asks her, 'Are you outside trying to get in or inside trying to get out?"

In loving tribute to the late Lucille Mericle –

Disbelief: Well, f—k me running! Housework: Ah gotta douche this place out.

Boxers Trash Talking

Back in the day when boxing was a more popular sport, there was a ritual called "the weigh in" which was largely a PR opportunity to give opposing fighters the opportunity to insult each other with impunity as they were weighed to make sure the boxer was the proper weight to fight in his class.

A weigh in for heavyweights was largely pointless because the only had to weight 200 lbs. + to qualify.

There were 14 categories for ranking the classes below Heavyweight. The least of them were called "Pi Weight" where participants had to weigh 97 to 101 pounds. The average size of an 8th grader, I would imagine.

Trash talk was a chance for the boxer to display his wit (if any) against his opponent. Shortlist.com has a compilation of these if you wish to pursue the humor farther. Meanwhile …

Mohammad Ali to Floyd Patterson, "I will beat this guy so bad, he'll need a shoehorn to put on his hat."

Mike Tyson, "My main objective is to be professional, but to kill him."

Willie Pep to a former opponent, "Lie down so I can recognize you

Chapter 7 – Movies and Martinis

Would You Order a $43 Martini?

Despite being a great fan and ardent supporter of the Dirty Gin Martini, I wouldn't spend that kind of money without it being a solid gold classic glass that the drinker gets to keep. And I'd bring a goldsmith with me to assay it right then and there.

Trust no one. Especially bartenders.

Epic Steak, San Francisco, is getting a lot of publicity for their new offering – the Fog Point martini said to be made from distilled San Francisco fog. The fog is not wisps escaping from the glass (as though the bartender had slipped slice of dry ice into the glass,) but instead it is "distilled" fog captured in filters mounted in trees at higher altitudes which drip, drip, drip into containers. Only about two cups per day are gathered which tends to jack up the price.

This "distilled" fog is then "filtered through premium wine" and turned into Fog Point vodka which, frankly, I think is a big bait and switch. You think you're getting potable fog; what you got was the shaft.

In fact, more insulting is the fact that what you are drinking for $43 is *fog sweat*. The bartender should write down the recipe and decamp to

London. They've got plenty of ground-level fog; no trees need be climbed in the collection of same.

A Quiet Movie vs. a Raucous Debate?

The 2016 political season has been particularly brutal for these events and I myself would rather creep down to Under-This-House and sit in the dirt, eating raw Brussel sprouts, reading the collected works of Alfred e. Neuman than watch one. You now know my position on politics.

Happily, Richie was able to keep me upstairs with a movie of his choice from our main library (an excellent source of free movies, by the way.)

He chose "Carol" adapted from the Joyce Carol Oates novel, "The Price of Salt."

This dubious bit of the film maker's art starred Cate Blanchett as "Carol," a woman trapped in a loveless (on her part) marriage to "Hart" Kyle Chandler and young "Tereza," Rooney Mara who becomes involved with the older (much older) Carol.

I was amazed to see how little acting the two women could do for 118 tediously long minutes. Blanchett limited herself to an icy aloofness (except when she went nuts and beat up her husband – several times) and Mara clearly has only two expressions – doe-eyed and not. The "not" is indistinguishable from the doe-eyed. Clearly Mara was a star student at the Olson Twins School of the Dramatic (and Not So) Arts.

Anyhow, Cate and Rooney embark on a mini-Thelma and Louise run after spending 'way too much time exchanging hot-eyed Meaningful Looks. I think someone pointed them at the camera and said, "Visualize a hot fudge sundae."

Her husband finally begins to smell a rat. *She and her best friend Abby sure spend lot of time together* and takes her to court for a divorce and sole custody of their 10 year old daughter named "Rindy" which I finally figured out must be the diminutive for "Miranda."

It's during these scenes in the lawyer's office where we finally get to see more of Chandler, the husband. Black hair, dark blue eyes ... tall, trim body... majorly hot. If this were real life I would deeply and seriously consider the women's mental disabilities, arrange for a nice restful time for them in an undisclosed location and take off with him posthaste.   I mean, I do have a taser in my purse and I could always make it up to him later ...

But alas, it was only a movie. Still (eternally rosy here) it did beat watching the debate. Nobody really yelled in the movie.

Chapter 8 – France 1

Intro – My best friend Michelle lives in France. Over the years, 45+, we have frequently visited her there. This time we would be arriving in Paris after the Charlie Hebdo attack, the Nice truck terrorist and, back in Paris, the attack on the Bataclan nightclub.

Michelle e'd that if we didn't want to come, she'd understand. But if we did come, she proposed, that we avoid Paris altogether (not a hardship; we've been there many times) and go north to the resort towns in Normandy – Honfleur, Trouville and

Dinner, Honfleur. The waiter is putting down the restaurant's ramp for the wheelchairs.

This seemed like a great trade for Paris as we'd never been to Normandy. So I e'd back, "Sure!"

Over the years, we've learned a few things about going there and what to expect when you are there.

Travelers Checks

Richie loves traveler's checks. They're not accepted in France unless the monetary unit is Euros. Thus, he and Michelle spent most of an afternoon visiting the various banks in a small town in Bretagne. "Non!" was said decisively when the tellers were presented with American dollar traveler's checks.

That's when he learned to buy them in Euros. He called his bank for Euro checks only to be told they don't do travelers checks any more. Neither did the credit union nor Triple A. The best he could do was to exchange cash for Euros.

Call the Fraud Squad

Prior to leaving the country, call all of your credit card issuers, ask for the Fraud Squad and when connected, tell them that you are going out of the country, to which country and the dates.

When I did it, I got an automated call back from Chase making sure that it was me that had called. All of this for an account that has zero balance because I've never used it. So why carry it? For places that don't take MasterCard, slip'em your Visa.

Planned Spending

Sit down with paper and pencil and figure out how much "small money" you're going to need. Small money includes:

Postcards and stamps; restaurants that are cash only (and there are more of them than you might think – or certainly like) tip for the hotel maid, bus/metro fares, beer money!

Excellent Service

In the event that you actually get some, you should know that almost all bars and restaurants add 15% for the server. Look for "Service Compris" somewhere on the bill. It's customary though to leave assorted change for him/her if the service was excellent or if you've spent most of an afternoon over a glass of lemonade in a sidewalk café. Note: French lemonade is: a highball glass with ice, a shot of pure lemon juice, a small pitcher of water and the sugar bowl which is filled with what look like fat straws, but are actually sugar wrappers. Mix up your lemonade to your taste.

Done all of the above? Secured your passport and serious cash in a money belt? Look for the kind that hangs down from your neck inside your shirt or sweater.

Check! Got your boarding pass? Let's go!

Chapter 9 – Flying to Paris for a Wedding in Marseilles

Air France #069, direct from LAX to CDG, Paris.

Departure at 6:45 p.m., arrival the next day at 2:15 p.m. French time.

The Major American Airline (MAA) no longer flies direct to Paris, so we elected to sample Air France's "Priority Status" which was just being introduced. They call it "Premiere Voyager."

"Priority" was certainly a first for us. Flying non-revenue (non-rev) generally means that we are the last to scramble aboard to grab the first open seat in Steerage, of course – I once got kicked out of 1st before I'd sat down even though I was right, 1A was vacant.

Air France's Priority Service meant we were welcomed in the AF lounge, gratis. This lounge also serves pax flying on Delta, KLM and Aeromexico.

After checking in at a counter, we saw that the lounge itself was a very large room with cubicles for computer users, comfortable tables and chairs and a complimentary bar (from soft drinks to Courvoisier) and various snacks such as cheese'n cracker packets, honey-roasted peanuts, olives and so on. They weren't doing much of a business; we were the only ones there.

We picked a table overlooking the runways and had a pair of Stellas and some peanuts. We knew damned well they'd feed us dinner so this was our *aperitif* moment. It was so still that the only sound was the faint hum of the air conditioning. Very different from being down at the gate.

We boarded and were shown to our seats 10 A & B toward the very front of the plane, but we were not in First – we were on the top deck of the A380.

After the mandatory flute of champagne we were served an "amuse bouche" (literally something to amuse your mouth) of bread stick bits wrapped in Coppa salume on a bed of blue cheese over German red cabbage in a bent-handled (plastic) spoon a la Thomas Keller, Chinese Laundry.

The appetizer was a generous serving of Maine lobster claw chunks and a mango salad.

Richie opted for the tournedos with a peppercorn sauce, carrots, Bok Choy and Jerusalem artichokes. I took the Cajun shrimp and spicy saffron rice.

We turned up our now patrician noses at the breaded young guinea hen, which were hen cutlets with Madeira wine sauce, potatoes Lyonnaise and broccoli flan.

The cheese course tray was passed, take your choice and then a trio of small desserts appeared and everyone got an apricot macaroon with lavender; a "blueberry delight," and a milk chocolate concoction with bergamot.

On we flew into the dark. With the sun came breakfast. Choices included a crepe filled with scrambled egg and cheese. A separate plate offered slices of Parma ham, smoked turkey, cheddar (!) and Provolone cheeses. There was a fruit salad with mascarpone cheese as well as every type of bread, croissant and *pain chocolat* you ever saw, served with pots of sweet butter and cunning little jars of jams and honey.

The female flight attendants (no males working our section) were all very sleek looking, with razor sculpted haircuts and beautiful skin; "skin" being one of the things French women seem to do effortlessly. They were a happy bunch and chirped like birds.

POSTCARD FROM FRANCE

Richie: Long flight; short sleep

Nina: Seats fold flat into a bed – 6 ½ hours sleep

R: Hotel, small, clean

N: We move tomorrow

R: Train was great!

N: Actually, it was! We drank beer all of the way from CDG to Marseilles.

Chapter 10 – Marseilles Hotels

The 30 Euro/Night Difference

Never having stayed in a Marseilles hotel prior to this visit, I had to rely on guidebooks and kayak.com to "see" the various hotels (and their prices.) Travel expert Rick Steves praised one as being relatively cheap, clean, great location and so on. He mentioned in passing that the hotel layout was a bit different.

Indeed it is. After entering the street door, you climb up two flights of steep stairs, lugging a roll-on and carry-on each. You will arrive panting – air conditioning is not wasted on stair wells and August in Marseilles is hot – at the reception desk. After signing in, you will heave your bags up another flight of stairs where you will find the elevator. Which took us up one (one) flight to our floor. Why it's all the way up there and not down on ground level where it would be useful, I will never know.

In truth, this building dates back to the 1800s and has been reconfigured several times in its long history. The floors tend to slope and gave me the unpleasant sensation of being a sailor on shore leave.

The room was so small that I'd later joke that I've been in bigger bathrooms – on a plane!

It was sparsely furnished, the "furnishings" being a very small bed and one battered wooden kitchen chair.

The selling point was the view from the one window. The Old Port is U-shaped and the hotel was located in the bottom of the U so we did have a lovely sprawling view of the Old Port.

It was very hot the night we arrived and since the a/c seemed not to be working, I left the window open. And we listened to traffic, sirens, car radios and drunks yelling until I finally got up and closed

Next morning we went down for breakfast in the lounge area. It was a nice spread – slices of deli ham, an egg cooker for do-it-yourself hard-boiled, croissants, butter, yogurt, dry cereals and apricot or orange juice.

Then we set off for a different hotel. I didn't fly all the way to France, ride the fast train all the way from the airport to Marseilles to sleep in the equivalent of a coffin.

Off on our stroll around the port after a right turn away from the old one, we popped into the first hotel we came to – Hotel La Residence (hotel-residence-Marseilles.com) and they had me at "Bonjour!"

Excited, I elbowed Richie. "Look! An elevator on the first floor!" A computer for guest's use. Wonderfully chill a/c (August in the South of France is hot, damned hot!) A chic restaurant (theirs) just outside the front door.

The clerk gave me the rate – 130 Euros/night and I asked to see a room. She handed me the key to 403; we promised not to touch anything and bounded on to the elevator.

The room faced the U with a splendid view from the solid balcony (not like New Orleans where balconies seem to be made of black iron lace) with a small table and two chairs. I could sit there and smoke contentedly – because smoking is forbidden in the room. But an ashtray and a book of matches were provided along with a little note earnestly pleading not to smoke in the room. Happy to comply!

Best of all were the four desk clerks during our stay. Three were very professionally dressed women; the fourth was the night guy who was very friendly and funny. The ladies were all long-legged (a trend in France) and thin. They reminded me of sleek greyhounds (who could use a phone and a computer.)

The ladies were of immense help – called a cab for us, showed us where to park the rental, answered questions about where things were; provided maps and logged me on to the computer every morning. All of these things were done with maximum friendliness and a genuine desire to be useful. They were so nice that when we visited Aix, I brought them back little boxes of Callisons (a type of local candy) as a modest "thank you." They were quite surprised.   Clearly, they thought they'd just been doing their job.

The breakfast help, a waitress and a young waiter were friendly and watchful. On our first morning, I asked for a glass of water so that we could take our pills. The next morning, he grinned and brought a pitcher of water to the table. "For the pills" he announced. Yes, that kind of attention to detail.

This outdoor terrace was a great place to butter a chunk of baguette, spread honey on it and eat it while gazing at the never-ending parade of people on the sidewalk.

Algerian mothers pushed strollers, on the way to the market; a chef was clearly headed for the fish mongers who sell right off the boat, pipe-smoking old men settled a little more comfortably in the woven grass chairs and read the newspaper. Concierges swept the pavement in front of their hotels (no lack of hotels.)

The seafood restaurants that crowd each other for prominence were being dusted off, chairs lifted off of the tables and arranged in order.

Everybody but me was doing something. I liked it there so much that I was only half-joking when I said I was going to move in and the hell with going home

AIR FRANCE 66 HAS LANDED

We were delayed for an hour coming out of Paris and delayed another half-hour on the ground at LAX. The aircraft was another A380 and the plane had to wait for one of the few jet bridges that reaches the 2nd story where we were seated.

We got home about 11 p.m. French time and are exhausted, but better to keep to regular hours than go to bed like I'd like to do.

Chapter 11 – You So Crazy!

Bigamist Marries 8th Tree – Hindustan Times

A Peruvian environmental activist named Richard Torres married a 1,000 year old tree in Oaxaca in May, 2016.

The ceremony, according to onlookers, was colorful. A photo sowed a gnarly-looking tree with a bridal veil twisted around it. Presumably this meant that the tree was in fact a virgin.

Torres, also an actor, seems to have forged something of a second career by traveling to various locations and marrying trees. This was his 8th venture down the aisle with a tree. Or, rather, up TO a tree. Previous marriages to trees have been neither annulled nor has any tree divorced him as far as is now known.

The "Comments" to this article prove once again the willingness of American citizens to work together in a creative way. Herewith I give you samples of their brilliant work:

"We'll call our first child 'Cord.'"

"I was in a sexual relationship with a tree … it was 100% heterosexual, but the tree cheated on me with the gardener."

"What a birch!"

"Thank yew."

She Thinks She's Precious

"I Was Told There'd Be Cake" by Sloane Crosley   230 pages $14

A collection of essays by Crosley wo is said to have written for Playboy, the NY Times, the Village Voice. Having tasted her cake, I have to wonder just how *many* articles she's written for any one of them.

She calls herself a "professional New York woman," and writes about the trials, tribulations and joys of living in Manhattan.

I noticed that the "professional New York woman" is going to be "Poor hapless (but adorable) me! Aren't I just the cutest little thing in shoe leather?" (pirouette.)

She warns of incoming "preciousness" in Chapter 1 – she tells dates not to bring her flowers, candy or wine, she wants a pony! Yes, a plastic My Little Pony and Me doll. She keeps them in a kitchen drawer and will often ask guests after dinner, "Coffee, tea or a pony?"

 (Ed. Note: are you gagging yet?)

Immigration and Customs Enforcement (ICE) Has Collectively Lost It

May, 2016   Alvarado, TX: ICE has okayed construction of what will be called the Prairieland Detention Center at a projected cost of $42 million. Said construction is being promoted as providing jobs for some 100 workers.

Alvarado is 26 miles south of Ft. Worth and is considered a nice bedroom community for both Dallas and Ft. Worth.

Construction of the Prairieland Detention Center is expected to be completed in November, 2016 (It apparently opened in January, 2017)

The facility will be offering 700 beds with a **36-bed, entirely separate section for ILLEGAL immigrant transgenders and their special needs.**

Texas, Texas … what done come over you – you're not the law-abiding Texas I've always known.

"Grotesque: Comically or repulsively ugly or distorted"

That's my thought about a new trend in the Body Enhancement folks who are deeply into tattoos and piercings. Mind you, I have no objection to it if others what to dive in both feet first. It's a free country; git'er done if you want to do it.

But this newest fad is deeply disturbing to me because a careless needle can spark a massive infection and leave you blind for the rest of your life.

I am talking about eyeball tattoos. I'll give you a minute to get over your reactions which would probably be "You can't tattoo an eye!" immediately followed by "EEEW!"

Apparently, it amounts to basically dying the white of the human eye a different color. Pale blue, navy and RED! For a devil's eyes! seemed to be popular choices.

Additionally, I learned in my research that the bony parts of the body – shoulder blades, upper shoulder, and neck – are the most painful to have tattooed as there are a lot of bones under the skin.

The soles of the feet and the palms of the hands are non-starters because both sites quite probably have calloused or thicker skin which over time flakes and sheds both skin and tattoo. Save your money and get a lip pierced or something

Chapter 12 – Kitchen Knives and German Speck

Do You Suffer From Knife Anxiety?

Or is the real truth the fact that you're too bone-idle lazy to live?

Whatever.

The Whole Foods store in New Bryant Park, New York, has among other delights such as a rolling cart dispensing made-this-very-minute! tahini dips or this: A blue neon sign above a spotless counter reads PRODUCE BUTCHER.

"But, but," you stammer in vegetarian horror, "Butchers deal only with (shudder, eye roll of desperation) "animals!" (Blows nose in organic cotton bandanna

The Produce Butcher is there to accept your head of cabbage or bunch of carrots or turnips or broccoli (little trees in family vernacular) and cut them as you require – chopped, minced, cubed – ready for the table, steamer or smoothie.

It won't matter to the wealthy health addicts, but this is NOT a free service on the part of Whole Foods. It's a dollar a pound for "bulk veggies" such as a head of cabbage or cauliflower.

This is not actually a groundbreaking service. Mario Batali's Eataly started doing it seven years ago. Since Whole Foods is promoting it like the best thing since crisp bacon – oops – I have to wonder what kind of a success or not it was for Eataly. I seem to remember Batali quit doing it.

One reader commented rather snide "E-coli Warriors?" Many others decried the persnicketiness of taking an onion to be dealt with and another asked if someone would be sent home with them to spoon feed these customers. "Millennials" was mentioned frequently. And not in a nice way ...

Many of us already know of this vegetable treatment. In restaurants, it's called "prep cook" and, yes, they do cook your meal for you. But I know of none that will actually feed your dinner to you. Attention Whole Foods – Money opportunity here...

Speck – It's Not a Spot on Your Windshield

Speck is smoked prosciutto and I'd never heard of it until I came across it as an ingredient in some dish in a food magazine.

Next day, there it was in the Trader Joe's meat case so I bought a package. To be frank, I'm not that crazy about prosciutto since it takes forever to chew it up enough to swallow it. But it does floss your teeth while you're chewing. Nothing is all bad.

Of course, I had no idea what I'd actually do with it, but it's always good to have hors d'oeuvres in stock. Then I was saved by the bell – literally. Bob and Pat invited us over to meet three of their grandsons along with two of their girlfriends. With a shout of glee, I accepted and grabbed the speck. A tasting panel in the offing!

The Speck Panel's ages varied; we had five men and four women, none of whom had ever tasted speck, but all of whom were familiar with prosciutto.

Hands-down we all preferred the speck. It has a tougher texture than prosciutto; it has tiny flecks of salt – much like dried beef. It was a darker red meat with a whiter fat (color contrast?) than prosciutto.

Belatedly curious about what I'd eaten yesterday afternoon this morning, I looked it up.

Speck originated in the 1300s in northern Italy and Germany when it was hung up to smoke inside the peasant's kitchen chimney.

Today it's "cold smoked" – never higher than 68 degrees in modern, well-ventilated facilities. Traditionally, it's smoked for two or three hours a day – for three months!

"Speck" in German means "lard" and comes from "bachen" or "bacon."

Mario Batali wrote about speck. A pork leg is cured in salt and a choice of flavorings – juniper, pine, cinnamon, nutmeg or coriander over a pine or juniper wood fire. Naturally he touts Speck della Alto-Adage, Italy, which formed a committee that oversees production and name rights and believes theirs to be the only authentic speck to be found.

Don't tell Trader Joe …

Chapter 13 – Write Stuff

Would You Go Without Bathing for Three Months – For Research?

"How to Be a Tudor – A Dawn to Dusk Guide to Tudor Life" by Ruth Goodman   320 pages $29.95

So that we're all on the same page here (rah ha ha!) the Tudor period existed from 1485 to 1603. Henry the VIII reigned and killed wives with some frequency during these years.

The book starts with the rooster's crow awaking the sleeper. There were only three cities; everyone else lived in the suburbs where they might keep a cow and certainly chickens. The sleeper who was poor slept in masses of straw on the floor; the rich had canopied beds – said canopies keeping the heat in during winter. I guess peasants just grabbed a handful of straw and stuck it into the cold place.

One of today's first thing in the morning tasks is to shower. But bathing in those days was considered extremely dangerous – not because of slippery shower floors; showers didn't exist; anyhow, rare was the person who bathed in hot water with soap.

And yet, personal hygiene was of primary concern. Smelling sweet and fresh was very important to the men and women of all classes. How did they attain this?

They used linen squares to scrub their dry bodies every morning. They did wash their hands and splash their faces with water. They also put on a clean pair of underpants every day.

As only the rich were well off enough to have a large supply of underpants, the poor had to make do with perhaps three pairs. The one being worn, one clean waiting and the third in the laundry. Underpants were often listed in the wearer's Last Will and Testament and given to survivors.

Goodman decided to try this and for three months she did. She remarked that while you might think the person would reek to high heaven, she didn't so, probably, they didn't either.

She wrote that clean teeth were equally important as a part of personal hygiene. Toothpicks were used at the table (Emily Post and Miss Manners would have fainted, had they been there.) Various powders (soot or salt or ground cloves) were applied with vigor to the teeth using the fingers or a small square of cloth.

Frankly I was very surprised to read this concern with personal hygiene as I had read that people Back Then never or rarely bathed and that everyone who couldn't afford perfume absolutely reeked with equally personal smells. It's "refreshing" to learn I was wrong. It's okay to time travel back to Tudor times! Crank'er up!

A Little Goes a Long Way...

"Andy Rooney – 60 Years of Wisdom and Wit" by Andy Rooney 286 pages $26.95

He was born January 4, 1919 (died age 92) and in the fullness of time went on to found a great career based on little more than being a professional curmudgeon. He was never caught without an opinion, no matter the subject.

He and Marguerite married in 1942 and had four children; three girls and a boy. She died in 2004 and Rooney was said to be inconsolable.

The book is loosely divided into three parts –
memoirs, essays on such as "Chairs" – he's for
them – the importance of everyone personally
taking their trash to the dump (Uh, Andy, few
cities have dumps any more) because we need to
appreciate what we throw away. The last section
is an accounting of what he specifically dislikes
and likes - "dis" beats "likes" to no one's real
surprise. Christmas made the cut; he likes it.

The book is interesting enough it you don't try to
read all of it in one day. I think of it more as a
browser book as in, "Well! Let's just see what
Andy Rooney thinks about that!"

Incidentally, if you've seen online lists of things
that he is said to have written – he didn't. He
would have loved to find their author though.

ATTENTION! WRITERS!

Listen to this! The body of a British children's
book author who was worth 4 million pounds, was
finally found in a "cesspit" in an old well in the
garage of her 1.5 million pound home. Her
dachshund Boris was found near her body. She
had been missing for three months.

The money didn't stop there. It is estimated that
Helen Bailey's monthly royalties were 5,000
pounds per.

Fiancé Ian Stewart, 56, lived with the 51year old writer. It is believed that he gave her increasingly larger doses of sleeping meds in her food/drink. She had complained in e-mails to friends to ask them why she felt so sleepy so frequently. The day after she signed a new will favoring him, and she was sufficiently doped up, he suffocated her, wrapped her in a comforter and blomp! splash . (The cess pit was full of human waste.)

Okay, it's a terrible story of human depravity, greed, avarice. Never mind all of that.

Did you see the important stuff?! A 1.5 million house, 4 million more in assets and 5,000 pounds/month royalties? All of that for a children's author? And little kids rarely have any cash on them!

Writers, we need to do some serious thinking about marketing. Meet next Thursday at 2 p.m.

When the "Other Woman" in Your Marriage Is ... Your Husband

"Sex Changes, A Memoir of Marriage, Gender and Moving On" by Christine Benvenuto   294 pages $25.99

Nutshell: Benvenuta and her husband had been married for 20 years and had three children. The citizens of their small town in New England (never identified) admired their "perfect marriage."

And then one night, right after having had sex, he turned to her and said, "I'm thinking constantly of my gender" a prelude to informing her that he now wants to live the rest of his life as a woman.

To say that she reeled in shock is understatement. The husband becomes a total narcissist, a sea change from being a funny, kind guy who was an excellent father to their children. All of a sudden, his life was more important and "meaningful" than those of his children.

He began to wear women's underwear under his Dockers and flannel shirts. He let his hair grow out. He had his facial hair lasered off.

His therapist, a trans-gender specialist, encouraged him, praising him for his bravery. His wife though was terrified that he would start wearing skirts and dresses in public, the last thing she wanted their kids to see. They were puzzled enough by his preoccupation with self and his lack of interest in their daily doings.

She makes a point of the attitude of the citizens there by calling their village "The Valley of the

Politically Correct." This translates to" everyone thought he was a hero, completely ignoring the fact that he was abandoning his wife and three children. That apparently didn't matter. They fell over themselves to prove that they were politically correct and supportive of him. So much so, that many of them chided *the wife* for not being supportive!

They stayed "married" and lived in the family home for two very long, secret-filled years before getting into a bitter custody battle over the children.

His father, a rigid stern cold man wanted his only son to grow up to be just like him. The son, terrified of his father, decidedly did not want to be just like his old man.

But … *if he were a woman, he couldn't be!*

It's an interesting tale and Benvenuda tells it well.

Chapter 14 – Touring a Mafia(??) Castle and Laughing at Death

Oheka Castle, Huntington, NY

Finding a castle on Long Island's North Shore seemed a rather unlikely possibility, but when digging around online for things to see, there it was in the guise of an extremely expensive hotel.

The guide on the tour we took ended the lecture with an offer to inspect a "typical" suite. At $1,800/night??? I didn't bother to go see it as our ship hasn't floated in to dock yet and instead repaired to the bar where the décor was homage to Charlie Chaplin. They were great friends. Oheka is a combination of the first owner/builder's name. O-Otto; HE – Hermann and KA for Kahn (I kept pronouncing it "Osaka.") Kahn spent five years from 1914 to 1919 building it. It took two years just to build the artificial hill it all sits on.

It is also the first totally fireproof home ever. Kahn's previous mansion had burned down which clearly marked him psychologically. Oheka is constructed with steel beams and the walls are 30 in. thick. New developers couldn't raze it to build something different. It wouldn't catch fire and the bulldozers couldn't penetrate the walls.

Originally it was the largest private home in America with 127 rooms covering 109,000 sq.ft. It was also, as ownership changed, a retreat for NYC Sanitation Workers which was a substantial step away from the glittering balls and gala dinners that the Kahns threw. Then it became the Eastern

Military Academy. A local told me that Donald Trump had attended the Academy.

See Oheka in these films – "Citizen Kane," "What Happens In Vegas" and has been the background for numerous videos

No 95 year-old mansion can escape lurid tales and Oheka has one.

Here's the back story: in 1984, a developer named Gary Melius bought it. Refurbishing it (it had been vacant for five years) didn't go well; he ran out of money despite having paid $1.2 for an empty building and the land underneath it. But, as time passed, Gary recouped his fortune, bought it again and spent the next 30 years returning it to its original 1919 beauty.

On the night of February 24, 2014, Gary was accosted in the parking lot and shot by a masked intruder. The villain of this piece has never been caught (or even found for that matter) but rumors persist that the gunman was either an inept hit man (the gun jammed after the first shot; a double tap thus forestalled) OR Gary's son or stepson were behind it. There were murmurs of Mafia justice (crime unknown) and unpaid gambling debts or a son's greed, but none have been verified. I used "Mafia" to make this piece more … interesting.

Apparently undaunted (or bills paid and sons financially satisfied,) Gary recovered and makes periodic tours of the premises to greet hotel and tour guests. That's certainly his prerogative; he's spent 30 years of his life putting it together.

A Light-hearted Look at Death

C'mon – get over yourself – we're all going to die someday. And I'm talking about every single living thing on this planet. Eventually.

If you believe that you will merely be transported back to your home planet, then go do the dishes or wax your driveway or something. This won't be of interest to you.

I think of death as the Last Big Adventure. No one has ever come back and described where they had been or what they had been doing, so why not go with the adventure theory.

That settled (for at least three of us) let us move to the fun stuff – the afters of your funeral. "Afters" is a word in common usage to describe the reception given attendees after you have been disposed of – with suitable lamentations, tears and wracking sobs, of course.

By the way, leave strict instructions that your remains are to be cremated to avoid nasty scenes at the cemetery when a grieving IRS agent/discarded mistress, etc. tries to throw themselves into the open grave with you. Posted signs reading "Single Occupancy Only" have proved to be less than effective.

So, you're in the ground, the last mourner has left, forgetting you by the time they reach the gate to the cemetery; it's time to party!

It's your duty as host (as it were) to provide an open bar, food and ensuing gaiety. Helpful hint: order the champagne servers to re-fill a flute even if it's only a third empty. Champagne may not raise any boats, but it works hellishly well on spirits.

Consider opening the karaoke session with a rousing rendition of Vera Lynn's "We'll Meet Again" which is perfect for this event and was very popular during WW2. Cheery, upbeat – all of the things you'd want to say to the crowd if you were there.

And make sure to have transportation arranged for inebriated guests. You don't want all of them piling in on you at once before you've settled in.

Chapter 15 – Food

Guest Editor

Big hand for Don, who was bred and born in Texas which in 2014 led the nation with 87.73 million heads of cattle. His wife has always raved about what a great steak he puts out. This is what he said to do.

"Buy the best you can afford. Beef is graded with "Select" being the least desirable and "Prime" the best. If you are astute and knowledgeable a good "Select" can be found. This requires patience and sometimes even that fails.

"Get a steak at least 1 in. thick and preferably 2 in. with plenty of marbling; I prefer bone-in cuts. Butcher cuts are not normally graded accordingly and if you know your butcher, he may show you the right path.

"I take the steak out of the fridge well before coming it. Tonight it will be out about five hours. I also salt and pepper at this point. I am not a salt fan, but beef should be liberally salted. Do not pierce the meat. The only seasoning I have had that was acceptable was chili pepper or coffee (dry, unused.)

"I cook on a gas grill. I wish I had a Jenn-Aire in the house, but, alas, I am impoverished. I prefer a wood fire, but for ease I use a gas grill. Cooking in an iron skillet is acceptable if you get the skillet hot enough, but you had better have the windows opening, fans going and be prepared for grease residue.

"I cook the steak on the hottest fire I can. I put it on the grill, let it sit for one or two minutes, depending on the thickness and do the other side the same. I cook only rare or medium steaks. I only cook them for others' sakes as I would sit down and eat the salted burger raw and warm. If someone at my house wants a steak well done or some such foolishness, I tell them to stop at McDonald's and get a burger on the way here.

"Last note: NO steak sauce is allowed."

Would You Make and Then Eat These?

Admittedly, one of the reasons I subscribe to Bon Appetit is to be awed and amused by some of the things the editors propose we eat.

When you've made an angel food cake or over-served Ramos gin fizzes, here's an idea for the leftover yolks from chef Christopher Kostow, of St. Helena, CA.

CURED EGG YOLKS

Make a bed on a dinner plate of 1 ¾ cups kosher salt mixed with 1/14 cups sugar and use the back of a big spoon to make egg-sized indentations in it.

Carefully place four egg yolks in the indentations, sprinkle any leftover mix across them, wrap the tray in plastic and store in the refrigerator for four days.

Then take them out, rinse under cold water, pat dry with paper towels and put them softly on a well-greased rack in a larger pan and put it all in the oven.

Turn on the oven to 140 degrees until they dry to the consistency of a firm cheese and let them cool. If your oven won't go that low, leave them in the cold oven for two days.

Now that you've got them – what to do with them? Chef Kostow grates them as a finishing touch for asparagus or shave over white bean crostini or crumble them over steamed vegetables or toss some in soup broth for more body.

You Don't Make the Crust, the Pie Does!

IMPOSSIBLE PIE

1 stick sweet butter, melted, plus enough to grease the pie pans.

1 ¾ cups sugar

4 large eggs

½ cup self-rising flour

2 cups sweetened, shredded coconut

2 cups of milk

Pre-hear the oven to 350 and butter two glass pie plates

Whisk the melted butter with the sugar, add the eggs one at a time and beat until the mixture is smooth. Stir in the flour, coconut and milk and divide the mix between the two pie plates.

Bake in the lower third of the oven for an hour or until the pies are firm to the touch and golden colored. Let cool completely before serving.

Almost as Expensive as Caviar

I'm referring to Trader Joe's Sweet Sriracha (uncured) Bacon Jerky which retails for $5.49 for a 2-oz. packet. To offer it to 10 people would cost you $54.90 which is rather steep if you are just drinking beer and watching a sporting event with sports enthusiasts.

Because I wondered how one could make jerky out of bacon, I bought a packet. It is good and ate 2/3rds of the bag when I got it home. It's a much softer chew than beef jerky. Because it goes into the drying oven well coated in a collection of sugar, honey and sriracha, it comes out sweeter than beef. Sriracha is not that hot a taste; don't fear it.

Corned Beef Tip

Factor's Deli, Pico and Doheny, Beverly Hills – we were ordering lunch after the annual visit to the accountant to get the taxes done. We always make this appointment so as to take advantage of the great deli food in Beverly Hills, but not here. We don't have enough Jews although I did do my best to keep Nate & Lizzy's in business. .

When Richie ordered a pastrami sandwich, the waitress asked him, "Hand cut or machine cut?" a question we'd never been asked before. "What's the difference?" I asked. She said, "Hand cut is thicker; the machine slices thinner" so, of course, you know what he asked for… "Hand cut, please…"

Odds and Ends

DRIED CHERRIES

Put a small bowlful near the Brie cheese – they go wonderfully together …If you don't like cherries, substitute a jar of fig jam – equally wonderful.

I stole this from Hudson House, PCH, Redondo. A bowl of mixed olives, cashews and almonds with a handful of dried cherries thrown in. The olive juice softens the cherries. This is delicious with drinks, but eat all of it as the cashews are soggy by the next day.

MY MOTHER'S SUGAR COOKIES

When I was a kid, we frosted them together. Then my sister came along (8 years difference) and they frosted them. Time passed, my sister married and her kids decorated the cookies made with the cutters our mother used. I remember a Christmas tree, a star, a camel and a hump-backed Santa with his bag of toys.

Here is how they made them –

3 cups flour

1 teas. Baking powder

1 teas. Salt

1 cup sugar

½ cup shortening (it's still made?)

2 eggs

1 teas. Vanilla (would double)

¼ cup milk

Sift together the dry ingredients, cream the shortening and sugar together and beat in the eggs.

Roll out and cut with cutters and bake at 375 for 8 – 10 minutes. Makes about two dozen cookies.

Alternative method: Buy raw sugar cookie dough pre-formed into cookie shapes at the supermarket and bake as directed.

DEBATE: RESOLVED SIL-PAT VS. METAL COOKIE SHEET

The advantages that silicon has: it doesn't melt easily (although it sure looks like it would) and can withstand 400 degrees. It's hard to stain. If a silicon tool falls into the floor of the dishwasher while it's running, it won't melt. Silicon is not porous. Unlike wood breadboards, it won't absorb germs.

A Sil-Pat baking sheet is used for baking and candy making. Since you don't have to butter Sil-Pat, you'll have less grease in the finished product. You'll never have to buy parchment paper again (and throw it out after one use.)

I visited chowhound.com and got opinions from people who do bake. To a person, they said that cookie bottoms crisp up better on parchment paper. They say they re-use the parchment until the whole batch of cookies is baked.

They all complained that Sil-Pat "felt slimey." When I asked Richie (the one who does bake) he said, "They're fine. No complaints at all."

WHITE PIZZA

My sister gave me this recipe as a Christmas appetizer and it's very, very good.

1 can Crescent rolls (Play-doh to me)

8 oz. brick of cream cheese

1 green pepper

1 red onion

8-10 pimento-stuffed olives

Spread out the triangles of dough in a pizza pan and bake as directed. "Butter" the bread with cream cheese. Cut rings of green pepper and red onion, decorate the pie. Slice the olives and dot where they would look good. Because you've made this with triangles of bread, it will easily cut into pizza slices.

GARLIC GREEN PEPPERS

This is great for a summer appetizer.

1 green pepper, cored and cut into long, thin strips.

1 or 2 garlic cloves, peeled, chopped and mashed with a spoon into about ½ teas.sea salt – do this

mash in the bowl you're going to serve it in. Add olive oil and toss in the green pepper slices - refrigerate until you serve it.

ADDING SNAP!

"Snap" in this instance means adding a little extra for "company food" such as tossing a handful of popcorn across the top of a bowl of tomato soup or taking three stalks of cilantro and making a little bouquet to be put on the side of the guacamole. This is also known as "plating" in restaurant circles.

Unfortunately, this is not "a good example" addressing you here. I have come across recipes for little crackers known as "Parmesan Crisps" at least three times; always thinking about how good they look; how easy they must be to make. And have never stirred my stumps, waddled out into the kitchen and made some.

But idly leafing through the new Food & Wines 2012 cookbook (foodandwine.com) a page made me jump back. It was a photo of Parmesan Crisps looking reproachfully up from the page. As in, "How come you don't like us? We're good; we're easy to make ..."

PARMESAN TUILES (tiles in French)

6 T freshly-grated Parmegiano-Reggiano cheese

1 ½ T sweet butter, softened

1 T + 2 teas. all-purpose flour.

Preheat the oven to 400, line a cookie sheet with parchment paper and set it aside. Make the dough and roll it into a tube (any thickness you want) and cut slices, put them on the cookie sheet, kind of softly flattening them on it. Put the pan on the bottom rack and bake for 3 ½ min, then turn the pan and bake another 3 ½ minutes.

They are said to be an excellent appetizer with drinks. If you're thinking to gift them, they will keep one week in an air-tight can.

Chapter 16 – Outings

Comb Your Hair, Put on Your Shoes – We're Going to a Wedding

INDIA: bring sunglasses. Indians are great believers in the use of VIVID colors. From the canopy to the guests' saris and furbelows. Is she blushing or is it just the reflection of her hot pink veil?

The groom, not to be outdone, will be equally flashy and makes his entrance riding a white horse with family and friends dancing around him. The bride and groom exchange garlands (more colors) and when the groom puts his garland around her neck, that means that she has accepted him.

IRELAND: The bride carries a little decorative version of a horseshoe for good luck. Back in the day, the poor woman had to carry the real thing. Imagine it – there she was in a white dress, a lacy heirloom veil ... lugging a Percheron shoe. Post-ceremony, glasses and forks are raised and the band plays Celtic music and step-dancers (hired pros for a big wedding) clack away.

ITALY: I've been angling for an invite to one of these for years! Post-ceremony, it's onward to the chosen restaurant where guests are often rewarded for their attendance with the presentation of a 14-course dinner! Well worth sitting through a two-hour Mass with Communion. The male guests all kiss the bride to make the groom jealous – never a good idea in Italy – and slip a check or cash-stuffed envelope into a bag the bride holds.

JAPAN: The Japanese have always preferred the low- profile life and weddings are no exception. Very often they were limited to only family and very close friends. Today they are much less exclusive. The happy couple believes that the guests bring good luck and so they reward them with mementos of the day such as chopsticks with the pertinent information printed on them.

KOREA: The ceremony usually takes place in the bride's home, but only after the prospective groom has presented a live goose to the mother-of-the-bride. Geese mate for life and he is showing Mom his intent. I think they could upgrade to a porcelain goose; the real thing is often tetchy and, in fact, they are used as farm guards in some countries.

Several days later, the now-married couple visit his parents who give them wine. The newlyweds give the parents and guests dates and chestnuts symbolizing the children they plan to have and the guests take them and throw them at the bride who attempts to catch them by holding out her skirt.

You were very, very good! We'll be going other places, too.

Visiting a Wine Cellar and Being Prepared

Food & Wine says:

Did you call ahead to see if they're open?

Make up a picnic lunch? (Never drink on an empty stomach. Trust me.)

Make sure you're carrying cash – many wineries charge a fee at their tastings, sometimes comped if you buy a bottle.

Leave the perfume and/or after shave at home. They mask a wine's aroma.

Hire a designated driver.

Avoid Saturday wine tastings – they're big with bachelorette parties and other rowdies.

Above all – don't get drunk. Pace yourself; if a wine appeals particularly, buy it and put in the trunk of the car. Go home and THEN you can swill and chew it around in your mouth to your heart's content.

At the Gay Thrift Shop

Pulling out of the garage at the gym, we were overwhelmed by the sight of a shocking-pink van emblazoned "Out of the Closet.org" tooling smartly down the street. What a cool name for a thrift shop!

When we got home, I Googled it and found that they also offered free AIDs tests, had a pharmacy and clearly catered to a gay clientele. The closest was located in Long Beach.

Instantly I e'd our friend Tone who is a long Beach resident, born in San Pedro. He knows that area like few could. He knew about "Out" – had even been in it once. One thing led to another …

Yesterday afternoon, we left our car at his house, hopped into his 4-door pick-up and embarked on the Tone Tour. "This corner used to have a fruit and vegetable market ... See over there? That used to be a bar..."

And speaking of bars, we rolled into his local pub for a refreshing pitcher of beer. After all, we'd been driving on a bitter cold and windy day for as long as 10 minutes! Hydration was clearly required.

After we all took our meds, we rolled onward. My excitement mounted when I realized that "Out of the Closet" was a gay charity. I had wonderful visions of rows of Great Big High-heeled Shoes, feather boas, frothing off of their racks; shelves of costume jewelry, sequined tops and tables of black mesh stockings lined up in a row. And groups of large men shrieking in delight, "Girl! That is SO you!" at their finds. A sort of roadshow version of either of the two "Cage Aux Folle's."

Reality was shockingly different. There wasn't a tranny in the place, but there were two Hispanic women quietly browsing through the women's section.

Richie and Tone picked through the men's stuff – a Polo here; an Armani there, but nothing stirred them to reach for their billfolds.

True, there were fancy cocktail dresses glittering in the windows, but they were probably left over from Halloween. The shelves of glasses, vases, bric-a-brac could have been in any old store.

It was a true thrift shop, indistinguishable from any Goodwill or Salvation Army or Children's Hospital. You cannot begin to imagine my disappointment.

Thrift Shop Finds in an Imaginary Store

A black t-shirt with this phrase spelled out in colored sequins: Drinks Well With Others

"Discover Wildlife; Teach School" picked out in "needlepoint" on a pillow.

Really rather special: "Horse Lovers Are Stable People"

Wall plaque: "A meal without wine is called 'breakfast.'"

T-shirt with a glass of red wine depicted: "They say one glass a day is good for you. They never said how many times to fill it."

Wall plaque: "Remember, as far as anyone knows, we're a normal family."

Wall plaque for women: "Cinderella is proof that shoes can change your life."

Wall plaque: "I smile because you are my daughter – I laugh because there is nothing you can do about it."

A black t-shirt with white letters that say, "I have discovered the Fountain of Youth and it looks a lot like vodka."

Chapter 17 – Spending Money

Pondering the Buys of the Crazy Rich

"W" magazine thoughtfully sent along a copy of their gift guide with this month's issue. In an excess of the cutes, each page has a different theme. "Show Me the Money" deals with emeralds, glittery clothing – a pair of gold lame hot pants for $795 for not enough material to cover your front and backside at the same time.

"Tech Support" offers black diamond mascara (you think you've got vision problems now –get some diamond grit in your eye) There are numerous black, white and silver items including a chair for $1,659.

"All That Glitters" advertises a Chanel dress for $42,300 (not a typo - $42,300.)

Don't forget the kids – the "Wild Child" is a page with such as this: baby-sized Diesel Jeans for $89. A True Religion t-shirt for your three-year-old for $44 and Gucci Velcro-fastened shoes for the one year old who is learning to walk and tie his shoes $295.

In my world (the real one) it goes like this: a summer baby wears a diaper and a t-shirt. A winter baby wears Target sweats. It is pointless to try to spiff up a baby. They just don't have the bodies for designer duds. Let's face it, the minute they are born, they begin eating and there goes a light birth weight and a slender figure. Better to buy something nice for yourself. You can appreciate it.

Irish Castle for Sale – 25 Bedrooms

Architectural Digest has given me some startling insights into the state of the economy. I think Ireland is going broke. All of a sudden there are numerous castles for sale all across Ireland.

Kiltegan – Granite Victorian domicile with 25 bedrooms, 17 baths (see what I mean about poor?) two half-baths set in 46,200 sq. ft. The building broke ground in 1867. Your $10.1 million will get you 427 acres of woods, two lakes, formal gardens as well as lodges, stables and cottages. Hmm… servant cottages? Are the servants (if any) being sold, too? Or will they be auctioned off separately?

A turn of the page gave us the chance to buy an island. Shared island, to be sure, but still …

Alexandra Bay, NY, known locally as Millionaires Row -mighty damned short row; only three houses on the entire island; is described as "just minutes away from the mainland by boat." Okay, that could be a cute feature in summer – sun shining, gentle breeze "Ooh, boat ride!" – but what about a howling gale in winter and you're out of brandy? Or cigarettes?

Anyhow, not likely to be our little frets. One of these three homes is for sale with this caveat: In need of significant restoration. The house – or what's left still standing (photo wasn't very clear) is still owned by the descendants of the original owner, one Alson E. Clark, an industrialist. It has 8 bedrooms and 3 baths (and I see a problem right away) and contains 4,700 sq. ft. in its three-storied shingle-type building.

Gnawing bitterly at my disappointment that it was not the entire island for sale, I misread the price and gasped out loud. $985 MILLION. But then as my vision cleared, I saw it was $985,000. As is.

No Eagles Were Harmed in this Experiment

"They're so tight they can make an eagle scream" is an expression used to describe someone who is so reluctant to spend money that they can make the eagle on a quarter scream in pain when it's pried from their hand.

Despite what this may sound like to you as it unfolds, I can assure you in front of God and two other responsible witnesses that the eagle on the quarter in my change purse never let out a peep. Not from July 10th to yesterday November 28th, a time span of four months.

My long-term windfall began innocently enough. Richie and I decided to go to Las Vegas for three days, beginning July 10th. To fund my gambling I withdrew five $20s from my account and stowed all but one of them in the back of my checkbook (which is an excellent hiding place for the folding green.)

I lost $4 at video poker bar at the Rio and I exerted so much effort winning it back (1 a.m.) that I really didn't have the energy to dip into my fund and gamble more.

Once home, the money languished, stuck in the pages of my calendar until we flew to Marseilles in August for a wedding. I wanted some walking-around money and Richie wanted to cash in some traveler's checks. We walked into the nearest bank and were politely told, "Oh, no, we do not accept American money ... and, Monsieur, no one in France will take your traveler's checks."

Richie is rather stubborn and he tried three more banks to no avail. So my $100 had a free tour of France. Again, it languished back in the calendar through September.

On October 11th, I took $40 with me to the jazz club and bought the first pitcher of beer ($14 with $26 left over.) At the end of October, we hit a couple of library book sales, but the grand total for that was maybe $6.50. I remember a couple of runs into the supermarket and paying cash for such as two sandwich rolls or a pound of hamburger or a can of corn. I paid $7 cash for a prescription drug.

Yesterday I was finally down to a dollar bill and a dollar's worth of change. Make no mistake, I can spend like a drunken sailor when I'm using a credit card (and, sadly, often have) but it takes me a long time to spend it when it's cash. I mean, cash is worth something, right?

An Odd Bit of Advertising History

"Just Do It" equals Nike in much of the collective conscious.

But many of us didn't know that it first appeared in TV ads in 1988, long after the guy who that said it had faced a firing squad in Utah.

Gary Gilmore, 37, was executed on January 17, 1977, for murdering two men; he was caught with the smoking gun in his left hand.

This is what happened next. Dan Wieden of Wieden & Kennedy Advertising was asked by Nike to give them a tagline for five very different 30-second spots. And the scene at Gilmore's death by firing squad popped into his mind. (The creative mind at work. Who among us is as gifted?) Gilmore's actual words were "Let's do it" and Wieden changed it to "Just do it." (Undoubtedly artistic license.)

Gilmore was a man of my own heart (except for the murdering thing.) Here is why: after the ACLU got him two (unwanted) stays of execution, he said, "They (ACLU) always want to get in on the act. I don't think they have ever done anything effective in their lives. I would like them all to just butt out. This is my life and my death."

The ACLU's two stays did affect Gilmore. After both of them, he attempted suicide. A man that liked his own way. And knew what it should be.

The First Century AD Detective

"Enemies at Home" by Lindsay Davis   342 pages $25.99

The Romans had an interesting system of justice. If a home owner was murdered at home and the guilty party was not immediately apprehended, it was assumed that one of the servants (which easily outnumbered family members) had done it and ALL of the slaves were promptly put to death.

A number of citizens worked as "private informers" and one of them was a young woman named Flavia Albia, the adopted daughter of Marcus Didus Falco, a former private informer. She has assumed his old job.

It is an unusual enough thing today – let alone 1st Century A.D. – to find a female investigator outside of a novel, but Flavia is called in to see who killed a rich couple, found strangled in the marital bed. Meanwhile, the understandably terrified slaves have fled to the Temple of Ceres which is a recognized haven for refuges.

Flavia is an interesting heroine, believable with a good sense of humor. It's an interesting book.

William Howard Taft. President 1909 – 1913

Not an auspicious beginning. His own mother told the press, "He is not my candidate. His is a judicial mind and he loves the law." Taft agreed with her, but wife Nelly had had visions of herself in the White House since childhood. She got her way.

She rehearsed her White House occupancy in the Philippines where she loved having all of those servants, five carriages and 13 horses. When her dream was finally reality, she brought a great many of her furnishings from the Philippines with her. So many that detractors started calling the White House the "Malacan Palace."

Taft was transferred from the Philippines to Secretary of War with Teddy Roosevelt's endorsement. Roosevelt said of him, "The most lovable personality I have ever come in contact with." Apparently, Nelly thought so, too; she insisted on riding next to him in the car taking them to the inauguration. It wouldn't be the last time she broke with precedence.

She made significant changes inside the White House. All of the ushers, who had been white men in frock coats, suddenly became black men in blue livery. Next, she ordered that male White House servants were to be clean shaven – Off with their beards and moustaches.

She not only changed the house interior to reflect her love of Philippine ornamentation and furniture, she took her decorating outdoors to create Potomac Park and then planted the famed cherry trees, which were a 2,000- strong gift from Mayor Ukio Ozaki, of Tokyo.

Despite Roosevelt's warning that the public considered golf a frivolous pastime, Taft insisted on leaving the entire afternoon off for golf. His vast weight (350 lbs.) hampered his swing as may be imagined. He used extra-long clubs, a "baseball" grip and used short, choppy swings.

He loved traveling for two reasons – it got him away from work AND Nelly's watchful eyes. Free from supervision, his appetite was sated. He set a presidential record for taking vacations. He would leave for his summer home in Beverly MS. With this instruction: Do NOT forward any mail to me.

Taft, due to morbid obesity, couldn't tie his own shoe laces; that was a job for his valet. When he got stuck in the presidential bathtub, it took two men to pull him out. He ordered a new tub that was 7 ft. long, 41 in. wide and weighed one ton.

Nelly did not go to Woodrow Wilson's inauguration. Instead, she sadly roamed around the private quarters until 12 noon exactly when she put on her hat and furs and walked out of the White House without a single word of farewell to anyone.

Chapter 19 – France – Getting There

The Relentless Personality Tour

Admittedly, I am too much of a Type A to travel well. Oh, fine for short hops like Las Vegas (plane) or Palm Springs (car) places where one can get home in a hurry if the need arises. The farther from home we go (New York, for example) the higher my stress level rises. LAX to Chicago to Dublin nearly killed me back in '06.

Now we're heading for the South of France for a family wedding (my French *famille deuxieme*) and I've had an upset digestive system for days. Part of it, if not all of my problem is that so much of travel is out of my control. Not good. I'm used to being in charge. And I'm used to (usually) getting my way. You can see why this train is edging into the suburbs of Disasterville.

But yesterday, while idly tapping a foot to the music and sipping a beer at the jazz club, I came to a stunning conclusion. I would handle what I could – keeping the tickets straight, the luggage close and Richie out of the train station bar – and leave all of the other matters up to God.

So: God is now in charge of whether the plane stays in the air - or not. He is charged with keeping the bullet train on the tracks – or not. In a plane at 47,000 feet or on a 200+ miles train, you wouldn't know what hit you anyhow. Michelle is a former flight attendant for Air France and when asked about any fears she might have, she laughed indulgently and said, "Oh, Nina – you only have time to think one quick Hail Mary!" she snapped her fingers. "Zut!" she said succinctly.

I have also tasked Richie with handling crazy French drivers and the traffic. He loves driving in Paris! He gets in, we buckle up (if ever you needed to, this is it,) starts the engine, revs it and bellows, "Bring it on, Frenchies! I'm from New York – show me what'cha got!" and we roar away.

Duties dispatched, responsibilities assigned, I can relax now.

Au'voir!

Or so I thought. Not a good start … Air France e'd and asked Richie to check in. There was no mention of me. I freaked, called the long-suffering Peggy at Zen Travel who told me that Delta – the Air France partner, in its wisdom, gave us separate reservations. No luck finding me there, so the hell with it; we'll check in tomorrow.

Leaving Monday on the 3:20 p.m. flight that lands at CDG at 11:10 a.m. Tuesday. It's 10 ½ hours there; 11 ½ home.

Today's exchange rate is 1 Euro = $1.14 US.

As have flown AF before and swilled down nothing but champagne the entire flight to Paris, have confidence that someone in catering at Delta knows I will be aboard and stocked the champagne cabinet accordingly. I've got the Valium in my purse.*

*Joking. My doctors don't trust me with Valium. They saw the profit I made vending the leftover OxyContins from hip surgery.

Airplane Food

I believe that one of the reasons so many of us look forward to a meal service on a plane is because it breaks up the often long expanse of time when we have to Just Sit There.

A good book helps; looking out the window at nothing at all is ...tedious. The movies are never new and usually imminently forgettable. The only interesting movie that I ever saw on a plane, and it held me rapt, was "Angela's Ashes" which is not exactly a laugh a minute.

So, when the flight attendants (FAs) come bouncing and clinking their carts up the aisle, we sit up and take notice. (In some cases, much like avidly hungry dogs.) "Ah, entertainment!"

Air France #065 LAX – CDG 3:25 p.m., arriving 11:10 a.m.

To commence – Marinated shrimp and scallops on a bed of ratatouille. Said ratatouille was a bed of raw, chopped peppers, tomatoes, celery and not the thick, cooked vegetable sauce we're used to having.

Entrée Choice of: Chicken with a mildly spicy red curry; jasmine rice with vegetables and Japanese furikake garnish (Richie's choice.) OR Shell pasta, lobster sauce, vegetables (my choice. The pasta was plump shells filled with, one hoped, lobster meat and not pollock

The Cheese Course – a variety of both cheeses and breads.

Dessert - Fruit compote and Grand Marnier almond cake

About an hour before landing, they served us breakfast on a tray which held: orange juice in those little aluminum cups with the peel-back top; a hard roll and butter. The roll was actually room temperature and not frozen! Blueberry muffin, plain Greek yogurt, strawberry jam. And a quarter piece of a grilled ham and cheese sandwich!

Air France #076 7:10 p.m. CDG – LAX arriving at 9:40 p.m.

To commence – smoked duck foie gras with mango chutney with lime and ginger sauce over baby spinach.

Choice of: Chicken with lemon sauce, bulgur with spices (mine) OR Spinach and ricotta cheese tortellini, creamed spinach and cheese. He was in the john. He loves spinach. I never cook it. So, I ordered this for him. He was furious; he'd wanted the chicken. There were some tense moments in seats 10A and B for a bit. I ate some sauce and bulgur and handed it off to him. This was not a sacrifice. Am not that fond of chicken and I really hate spinach.

The Cheese course – Camembert

Dessert was tropical fruit salad (Hmm, leftovers) and a vanilla streusel cream puff.

Again, about an hour before we landed, they passed amongst us with more food, but for the life of me, I can't remember what it may have been. I'd been deeply asleep and all I remember today is a lovely, hot cup of coffee.

Chapter 21 – The French Laugh at Me, Lunch at the Garden Supply place and the Hotel Cat Who Loved Us

The French, collectively, have long been accused of being humorless. And to strangers, they do appear to be that way.

Aside from gossiping about others, they have largely confined themselves to making fun of us outsiders. All you can do to *not* be laughed at is to be French. And I don't think you're particularly safe there.

As a "sale americain" (dirty American) I got my share of laughs; directed, of course, at my talents – apparently none whatsoever - at speaking French. I'm at a loss to understand this as I understand every word I am speaking. Perhaps they all have hearing problems?

The first insult came winging my way as we were having a nightcap (beer) at the hotel bar in Honfleur. We and the bartender were the only visible signs of life in the place, so I genially addressed him in French.

Whereupon, he sparkled a smile and asked, brightly, "Would you like to speak English?"

On another occasion, the three of us were having lunch at the Italian restaurant in Parly 2, the enormous shopping mall next to the hotel.

Michelle ordered a vegetarian pizza and to say the vegetables were "sparse" is gross overstatement. I ordered the gambas (prawn-sized shrimp) in Pernod sauce and Richie the scalloped veal. Scalloped veal is not photogenic being a sort of light grey. It is not appetizing.

All of these came with a salad which in France is largely a collection of lettuces unknown in America piled in a corner of the plate, sometimes with a sad little unassuming drizzle of salad dressing across them. Not so that day.

I reached for the olive oil bottle in the cruet with the balsamic vinegar. It was slippery and it slid out of my fingers to score a direct hit on the top of my full water glass which promptly exploded like a bomb. Glass shards few everywhere and water cascaded on to the floor.

Displaying the well-known and justly-famous *sang froid (cold blood)* for which the French are famous, none of the people around us reacted with shock once they'd gotten up from underneath their tables. The manager, however, nearly had a heart attack and became even more hysterical as he directed servers with napkins to mop up the mess.

Order was restored and lunch was served. I had to learn the hard way (again) that ALL shrimp in France are served "peel and eat" style. The shrimp arrive in front of you with heads, legs and feelers. Consequently, peeling and dissecting it takes time. Michelle was pensively eating pizza crusts and Richie was mopping up the sauce on his veal before I finally finished eating.

As there is never a hurry (that I've ever seen) in a French restaurant, I went out for a restorative cigarette. On my return, I and everyone else entering had to open our purses or shopping bags for a security guy just inside the front doors.

After the others had marched on past, I approached the guard and said (in French,) "Excuse me, I know it's none of my business, but … are you looking for a specific person?" and he drew himself up even taller (and he wasn't short to begin with - Senegalese) and said, icily, "Madam, I don't speak English."

I slunk away back to my seat at our table and then indignantly related this insult, but Michelle and Richie only laughed and laughed. Not quite the tears running down the face, hiccupping laughter, but damned close.

Far too enthusiastic for the event in my opinion.

Lunch in the Garden (Supply)

This was our first and subsequently only time to ever have lunch in the middle of a nursery and garden supply facility. Les Fermes De Gally.com is just such a place.

We rolled in on a graveled road and parked outside a complex of sheds, outdoor flower tables, braces of young trees and a large building which turned out to hold the restaurant, a gift shop, bathrooms and delicate plants such as orchids.

The restaurant – first stop, of course – is one of those "living room" places like some coffee houses here. In this case, the dining room faces a large picture window, but you won't be seeing rolling hills and a rushing river or anything even remotely scenic. Instead you will be looking in to a furnished living room (for humans) with a band of chickens happily disporting themselves in it. The lamp shade was somewhat streaked. This display was making a great hit with the kids present, who clustered around the glass, cooing at a favorite chicken who, typically French, ignored them choosing to peck desultorily at the seed

The menu is rather limited. "Do you want potatoes or eggs?" asked our server. Either choice involves cheese – such as batons of a very hard cheddar or melted raclette –

It was served with long slender spoon on the right – it's for scooping out the potato innards

saucisson, prosciutto, ham or pate. All of the egg dishes arrived boiled in the shell. The tables are rather closely set together so on the left and right happy diners were dispatching eggs by whacking them across the borderline of the egg cup they rested in and digging in. This seemed rather savage to me seated as we were near the chicken's living room window. A bit thoughtless to do that before the mothers, I thought.

The usual garden supplies took up a great deal of space and wandering along, we turned a corner and found ourselves in an area that sold live chickens of all varieties as well as fat, healthy-looking rabbits. "Surely as a pet," I thought. "Not a future dinner…"

We had dawdled over our lunches and now the promised storm had arrived. The rain boomed down on the tin roof over the plants; the chickens rootled around in their seed dishes and the rabbits curled up a little tighter. We fled to shelter and waited out the storm, merely a passing cell.

We emerged from shelter into bright sunshine and went home.

The Hotel Cat and Her Staff

It was an infamous day when the French outlawed smoking in a hotel. At the Ibis, Parly 2, you skip out the door of the breakfast room onto a huge patio with young trees in giant pots. It is admittedly a pretty place but not as attractive what with a howling, icy wind hurling across it. That is where smokers are sent.

So – I perched quietly on a tree tub edge and thoughtfully regarded my surroundings.

Movement to the right caught my eye as a small black cat came tentatively out of a low hedge, sat down and looked at me. I nodded and continued to look around. You have to ignore a cat; they can't stand not to be the center of attention, and they will come right up to you to get it.

Sure enough, after a couple of moments of scrutiny on her part, over she padded. I extended a fist for her to sniff and then petted her a couple of times. Cigarette done, so was I. It was very cold out there. She followed me to the door, but stopped short of it and sat down in the porch corner.

Her food bowls were empty and she began to groom herself so I knew she'd been fed. We became friends, largely I don't doubt because I would give her tiny pieces of cheese smuggled from my plate.

When we went to the supermarket on a beer run, I hunted out the cat food section and bought her a tin of salmon and a can of rabbit for our cats – I wanted to see their reaction.

Back at Michelle's I tore a sheet of paper out of my note pad and wrote, "A Mlle Ibis a votre amies en Amerique – Minuit, Fred and Rayon." ("For Miss Ibis from your American friends, Minuit, Fred and Streak") and taped it to the can. When we got back to the hotel, I stopped at the desk to give it to the day manager.

Who promptly went into a fit of near hysteria, reassuring me that the hotel feeds the cat! You would have thought I'd insulted his mother or something. He whirled around, disappeared behind a curtained doorway and re-emerged with two bags of dry food, each a different brand/taste, which he shook in my face, whirled again and this time returned with a stack of 8 to 10 cans lined up along his arm. Looking around furtively, nearly dropping a couple of the cans, he said, "We can't put the slices of ham on the buffet out again so she gets them, too!"

I made an envious face and said, "How spoiled!" and he drew himself up proudly and said, "Ah, oui, Madam – she 'as a staff of four!"

As I walked away laughing, I suddenly remembered the amount of ham offered at the buffet. It wasn't very much. "Feeding the cat is all very well, madam, but this is a hotel – if the guests want more ham, we will be happy to put more out. We are not feeding the cats of LeChesney." I could just hear him saying it.

Chapter 22 – Leaving France

Michelle drove us to Charles DeGaulle (CDG) airport in plenty of time for her to make it back home and not have to do needlework or read a book in the parking lot of rush hour traffic on the A13 *periphique.*

We had a 7:10 p.m. Air France flight home. When we checked in at 3:30 p.m. we could amuse ourselves until 6:30 when we could board.

My paperwork from Delta, Air France's ride share, informed me that I had a $200 credit owed me. I offered it to the Delta res agent who sent me off to another Delta counter where the lady told me it wasn't enough to upgrade to Business and anyhow, Business was full on our flight. Quickly I thought; shamelessly I begged. Instead, perhaps we could cool our heels in the Air France lounge? Oh, no, the refund is only for a ticket on Delta.

Neither one of us has ever flown Delta; they don't go where we want to go. Somewhere that $200 is floating around. Since it was an abstract anyhow ... *tant pis.*

We did ask for a wheelchair at the first res agent we had visited and he cordially invited us to go sit in the Reserved For Cripples area to wait for the wheelchair person to take us to the gate.

Bringing our wheelchair was a stroke of genius if I do say it myself. The wheelchair guy pushed me in an Air France chair; Richie pushed ours with the two carry-on bags both of which weighed enough to sink the Titanic; no ice berg needed.

Bonus points: CDG is so huge, so convoluted that we would still be wandering around looking for our gate were it not for the AF chair pusher. Up elevators, across expanses, onto another elevator and down. Repeat several times. There are separate elevators for wheelchairs and attendants only and they are all one-chair sized.

But first we had to do Security where something on my person set off the alarms three times. In France, they don't use a wand, they use their gloved hands. It's a man for a man; a woman for a woman. They are not shy. She went where no stranger has gone in quite some time and never another woman. I began to wonder ... maybe she's going to offer to buy me a drink when I'm cleared?

Finally, it dawned on me that it was the artificial hip! This occurred to me after handing Richie my watch and preparing to do battle about handing them my wedding right. AF had those machines trigger tight.

The nice pusher took us to Gate 22 and departed after showing me the about-every-three-gates Smoking Areas! CDG admits that people still smoke! Believe me this would be headline news at LAX.

Granted these smoking areas are glass cages, approximately 10 ft. long by 4 ft. wide with a rapid air exchange system. At one point there were five women in there with me.

Left on his own, Richie found a liquids shop – various coffees, soft drinks and beer taps. He got us a couple of large beers and we had a nice relaxing wait at a little table next to a window overlooking the runways. We finished our beers, our boarding call reverberated through the speakers and we were off.

Chapter 24 – Over on the East Coast ...

A Gift of "re-purposed" Toilets

The waters around Jamaica Bay, New York (I think it's on the flight path in and out of JFK) will shortly be the gratified recipients of 5,000 recycled porcelain toilets.

The toilets will then receive a filling gift – 50,000 oysters to be dumped in their bowls. Both porcelain toilets and oysters are said to be cleansing agents, in this case presumably the waters that cradle them.

Bonus points: the toilet-oyster mix is believed to be able to buffer New York from storms, clean the water and create a wildlife habitat. But don't drink the water there for a couple years, okay?

An Italian Wedding ... and Dreams

Since 1972 when "The Godfather" came out, I have longed to be invited to an Italian wedding. Who can forget that wedding reception?

Ah, to have been a guest – an absolute feast, wine flowing like water, and people all the way from babes in arms to great-grandparents singing, dancing, laughing ...

But. There's always living vicariously and until dear friends Red and Barbara went to one, that was all I had. A long-ago memory of a movie wedding! Hardly satisfying. But better than nothing.

Barbara told me all about it yesterday. Held in a catering hall on Long Island, the elegance began in the lobby – she said it was all marble and gold trim, with a sweeping staircase, a massive arrangement of real flowers...she said there was an enormous chandelier, too, glittering far above their

heads. Unimpressed so far, I mumbled, "Vegas."
And she said, "Yes!"

And went back to her description. "There were
cocktails and an open bar with every sort of
appetizer that one could ever wish. There was a
nearly life-sized rowboat filled with shrimp, clams,
crabs, lobster ..."

As she and Red were recovering a bit from all of
this – wait for it! – *the martini bar came down
from the ceiling, complete with a live bartender,
casually polishing a glass.*

She listed some of the things they'd eaten at the
eight-course dinner. "I had crab cakes to start,
then the pasta course was served, then the salad
and then the entrée – that was a choice of filet
mignon, salmon ... (sigh) on and on it went.
(remembering a detail) Oh! And the dinner
napkins were beige satin! How impractical is
that?!"

"At the end, they had this train? Row? Of tables
with your choice of gelato or pastries, coffee,
Amaretto – a whole bar full of after-dinner
drinks... it was wonderful," she sighed with
pleasure. I didn't say anything, lost in dreams of
all that as I was.

So! Here's the deal – if you are going to marry someone of Italian descent, CALL ME! I'll make it worth your while! I promise.

Chapter 25 – People Behaving Badly. That's Not My Gun Under the House! And Why It'll Never Be My Gun

Some Reading Material (if they can read) for the Thugs in #BLM

Until someone wised me up, I thought BLM meant Bureau of Land Management. My error.

Poetess Dr. Maya Angelou wrote this specifically for the National Council of Negro Women, founded in 1935 by Mary McLeod Bethune. It was used in **"The Black Family Reunion Cookbook – Recipes and Food Memories,"** from which I quote.

BLACK FAMILY REUNION PLEDGE; Maya Angelou

Because we have forgotten our ancestors, our children no longer give us honor.

Because we have lost the path our ancestors cleared, kneeling in perilous undergrowth, our children cannot find their way.

Because we have banished the God of our ancestors, our children cannot pray.

Because the old wails of our ancestors have faded beyond our hearing, our children cannot hear us crying.

Because we have abandoned our wisdom of mothering and father, our befuddled children give birth to children they neither want nor understand.

Because we have forgotten how to love, the adversary is within our gates and holds us up to the mirror of the world, shouting, "Regard the loveless."

Therefore, we pledge to bind ourselves to one another:

To embrace our lowliest,

To keep company with our loneliest

To educate our illiterate,

To feed our starving,

To cloth our ragged.

To do all good things, knowing that we are more than keepers of our brothers and sisters. We are our brothers and sisters.

In honor of those who toiled and implored God with golden tongues and in gratitude to the same God who brought us out of hopeless desolation – we make this pledge.

That's Not My Gun!

THE CURIOUS CASE OF THE GUN UNDERNEATH OUR HOUSE

Nancy Drew (me) and Ned Nickerson (Richie) were on it but too much time had passed. Now they would never know who planted a pistol in the opened yellow suitcase in the crawl space under the house.   ***

Two days ago, ,Ned had come upstairs and told Nancy, "There's a gun in your old suitcase under the house."

Nancy's eyes bugged out unflatteringly and she said, "What? (beat for consideration) "It could not be – or ever have been – mine. You *know* how I feel about guns!" (Nancy has a well-known pathological horror of firearms.)

Ned shrugged. "All I know is that it's down there. I think I mentioned this to you before.."

"Well, what did I SAY?" shrilled Nancy. "Dunno," Ned said. "Don't remember."

"You didn't touch it, did you?" Ned look scornful and said, "Of course not."

"Let's go – I want to see it," and grabbing the phone to photograph it, if a chain of evidence was called for, she followed him down the stairs and into the back yard.

After some difficulties getting to the open suitcase due to the piled-up boxes, bits and pieces, they bent over it. Using the back of his hand, Ned shoved aside the heaps of old letters, memorabilia, etc. aside as much as he could and unveiled The Pistol.

Nany studied it from a safe distance from the butt end of the gun. "I've never seen a pistol that *black*," she muttered to herself. "Looks like a .44 long?" to Ned.

Ned just shook his head, "You know I don't know anything about guns."

"Well, you were in the Navy; didn't they teach you about guns in basic training?"

"One day maybe, but you don't need a gun on a ship – they have enormous guns – why would anyone want a pipsqueak gun? Guns were only used for being on duty or Shore Patrol. Land stuff."

"Okay, I'll go call the police to come and get it. We've had quite a few contractors and gardeners who've had access to under the house through the years – perhaps one just stashed it here? Good thing we didn't touch it – fingerprints – and it *could be a murder weapon*," she hissed and went upstairs to call the police.

In her brief call, she stressed that since it might have been down there 30 years, there was no hurry in sending an officer out to the house to get it.

And Dispatch did take their time. Ned and Nancy cooled their heels by sitting on the tail gate of the truck and looking up and down the street.

Finally, a cop car pulled up, the officer turned on the blue and yellow lights and came ambling down the driveway to them.

He and Ned went to the site. Nancy waited for them to come back which they did rather rapidly. Nancy looked anxiously at the office who said only two words: BB pistol. Nancy mentally whirred through the photo album of guns she had seen and a "BB pistol" wasn't one of them.

"What should we do with it?" she asked the officer. He said, "Put it in the trash," lumbered back up the driveway, got in the cop car, turned off the flashing lights and drove away.

Nancy and Ned looked at each other. Nancy said, "I don't want some trash guy to find it .. we'll have to put it in a brown paper sack or something."

Ned said, "I'll take care of it – I'll put it in the bag with the used cat litter."

Nancy and Ned were disappointed in the outcome – visions of solving a 30-year-old mystery drifted sadly away.

A BB pistol. And no idea who put it there and no way to ever find out. They would never know after Thursday which is trash day for their street.

And Why It'll NEVER Be My Gun

I don't doubt that there are a lot of people who could say, "Well, I was brought up with guns and I think (opinion expressed here.) Like them, I was brought up with guns, too.

My father grew up on a Midwest farm. Most farms had some sort of firearm – for seasonal bird shooting, having to put an animal down…all practical purposes. To say nothing of deer for the table.

My Dad enjoyed hunting and with his cronies would take off for Wyoming or Colorado in deer and elk season. My mother teased him that they drank more whiskey on those jaunts than they did hunting.

Venison is terrible, but elk burgers weren't too bad. The deer skins were sent out to be tanned and mother made us deerskin jackets which were buttery supple.

I welcomed the gun cleaning ritual and can still remember the smell Hoppe's No. 9 Gun Oil, much like Proust's Madeleines. Daddy would brag all over again about his mighty kills, the devastatingly bad weather encountered; we had a fine old time.

His sister and her husband lived on a farm outside of Yates Center, KS, down in southeast Kansas. We visited them often.

I was a curious, restless child and loved exploring the farm's fields and meadows all by myself when I was six. Daddy gave me a beat-up old .22 rifle to carry on these expeditions. He taught me how to carefully slide the gun under a fence, barrel away from me, to then walk a few paces away, hold the barbed wire apart and get through the fence. My mother was horrified, but Dad convinced her he'd drilled me in gun safety. It's more than likely the rifle wasn't even loaded, but I loved the "big girl" thrill of being ready for anything! Bring it on! Fear of guns? What're you talking about?

By the time I was eight, I was allowed to sit with Daddy and his friend Orrin Blinn on the bank of a river near the Blinn's house, and plink leaves floating past us with a .38. Fear of guns? Huh?

When he went skeet shooting, it wasn't nearly as much fun pulling the trap. It was an honor at first, but first got old quickly.

When I was eight or nine, we were visiting Aunt Vera and Uncle Floyd's farm. Grandma V. his mother, lived "in town" (pop. 1,200 maybe.) The farm was some 12 to 15 miles out in the country and appropriately, Aunt Vera had named it "Land's End."

Daddy was driving us back from town after Saturday errands when he spotted a hawk, flying over a field. He slammed on the brakes (no traffic, country road), jumped out of the car, grabbed his new .247 Roberts with a scope sight out of the back seat and, taking aim, fired. Down dropped the hawk. We went off to see the damage. The hawk had been carrying a chicken away and both were now barely distinguishable as having once been birds. Daddy was quite pleased that one shot had brought them both down. I was glad to get back into the car.

The next traumatic incident that finished scarring me forever re guns was this. There was a pond across the road and Daddy decided we should go cottonmouth snake hunting. He carried a .38 Smith & Wesson.

We went safely under the barbed wire fence per previous instructions and started across the field to the pond where dwelt the cottonmouths. At the pond bank, we sensed movement and looked up to find a cottonmouth swimming directly towards us – quickly he shot and killed it – and in the same moment, we saw another snake heading for us from the underbrush. He shot and killed it, too. After making sure they were both good and dead, he cut a stout stick and impaled the bigger snake on it and we went back to the farmhouse driveway.

Once there, he got mother to take a picture of me, holding the dead snake on the stick. I was terrified because I believed that a snake wasn't dead until its head had been cut off. Daddy gloated because the snake had been pregnant and was carrying six egg sacs. Seven dead snakes. I was glad.

But the point of these two stories is that I have seen up close and personal exactly what damage a gun can do and I never, ever want any part of that.

Chapter 26 – Hello, London! (We Don't Always Go To France) ((It Just Seems That Way))

Both of us have wanted to spend some time in London for a long time. We have been there but it was a half-hour layover on a change of plane from LAX to Paris. Not even time to raid the duty-free...

When the parents of dear friends, obviously instantly smitten with our charm and good looks (as we were with theirs) invited us to come visit them at their home in the Dales, we decided to kill two birds (bad analogy; we were flying) and see London, then go to them and then straight back to Heathrow and home.

British Air (BA) was offering the same sort of upgraded Coach; down-graded Business that Air France had, so we bought the tickets to London.

At Tom Bradley International, we made mandatory stops at two different show-your-passport podiums, followed by security and bag x-ray. British Air boards from the back of the plane; none of this nonsense about putting First and handicapped on first.

Each seat held: a plastic-sacked small blanket, a pillow in a sturdy fabric case, an antimacassar for the headrest (to avoid hair oil on it?) The back of the seat in front of you has a button to pull forward on which to hang your coat.

The flight attendants all wear WW2 hats – the kind worn back then which is a sort of half cap/half beret designed to ride cockily on the side of their head and partially encase the French twist of the hair beneath it. I almost expected to see the odd Jerrie flying directly at us. What with the hair protectors, hats and general sullenness of the FAs it did seem possible.

After take-off, the drinks cart eventually came rolling through and I will never forget the "Bloody Mary" I was given. Plastic glass with two ice cubes, a mini bottle of vodka and a can of Campbell's Tomato juice. That was it. It was ghastly. Little did I know, this was merely the opening shot across my bows of what is found in British bars. Stick to a pint would be my advice today.

Dinner – everyone in our class got the same starter (Brit speak for appetizer) of a mixed green salad with a balsamic vinegar dressing. The Mains (we call them entrees) Choice of:

Seared filet of British beef (after mad cow disease scares, am not sure just how good an idea it was to label it like that) with port wine sauce, creamed leeks, roasted pumpkin and roasted new potatoes OR black truffle tortellini with chestnut sauce, roasted morel mushrooms (huge portion) and dessert for all was a slice of strawberry swirl cheese cake.

For breakfast we were each given a box containing a cold croissant, no butter, strawberry jam, a small sack of dried cranberries and a "health bar" that looked and tasted as if it had been made out of particle board.

After an uneventful landing, a brisk trip through Immigration and then into the arrivals gate where we bought an Oyster card each. These are the universal passes for the Tube, buses and consist of a blue and white card that you slide, face down, over a fat button that then opens the gate to let you into the trains. They were 20 pounds and the usual fare with cash would have been 1.44 pounds ($2.16) Do not forget to swipe it again before you leave the train area. If not, the Tube coppers figure you are still somewhere in the system, riding aimlessly around and around and around and go on a man hunt to find you.

I wondered a great deal "Why were they called 'Oyster' cards?" until it finally dawned on me – an old song "The world is your OYSTER." "Heh heh," I laughed.

Cards in swipe position we got on the Tube to Earls Court, our stop. We found the Rockwell easily enough, inquired about the nearest place to get a traditional Sunday lunch, were told, left our bags in their care and took off for the Stanhope Arms, a bar restaurant.

O/T We enthusiastically recommend theRockwell.com in South Kensington. We asked for and got a Garden Room and you can see our actual room at their Website – click on "Garden Rooms" and it will pop up first. I loved the little private patio with two garden chairs and a table and a couple of tubbed trees.

The Stanhope Arms was destined to become our pub of choice. In addition to an extraordinarily good slab of beef with gravy, Yorkshire pudding, boiled potatoes, the waitresses (drinks and food) were cheerily welcoming.

The Aussies, at the bar, were happily watching a soccer game with encouraging roars from time to time. A soft rain pattered down and we were all cozy inside, bellies full of beef or beer or both.

We reluctantly tore ourselves away, out the front door and up the steps of a massive, bright red Hop On, Hop Off bus. \This is a good deal – you pay one fee for two days of hopping on and then bailing when there's something you want to inspect more closely. That first afternoon, we stayed on the bus just taking it all in and getting an orientation as to general directions.

Visiting Queen Victoria Who Would Have Snubbed Yanks Like Us

The next morning we Hopped On, Hopped off and made some small purchases at Harrods, not forgetting to stop by the Diana and Dodi Memorial Display. The triangle contains the champagne flutes they were using when Dodi gave her the ring (next to the flute base.)

Then back on the Hop-per and endured an endless ride around London. We passed Picadilly Square three times! Finally, we got to the Kensington Palace stop, facing a gently sloping upwards dirt road that looked to be at least a mile long. In a gentle rain. Bladders bursting. Happily this eventuality must have been planned and to our left were a pair of rustic bathrooms tucked in beside a rough stone wall.

We weren't there to see Diana artifacts and just as well. The only trace left was a misty-looking head shot of her in a room crammed with current Royals portraits.

We were there (or at least I was) to see an exhibit on Queen Victoria, who was born there. It was very much drama (several actors in period costume) over substance.

They have a funny law there in that Richie paid 16.50 pounds admission, but I got in on a "concession donation" for 13.50 pounds. Once in, we went directly to the museum café where we split a very nice prawn and rosemary sauce sandwich from a grab-and-go sandwich bar, a bag of crisps and a bottle of water.

A slight note of criticism. British "crisps" are not. They are softer than our potato chips and the bag of "sea salt" crisps must have only been exposed to a passing wisp of salt air.

Kensington Palace disappointed. We'd been expecting a sort of mini-Buckingham Palace, but either George II and his crew lived very simply or the Kensington Palace people cleared everything out in an effort to have changing exhibits.

It was this kind of showmanship. A long cushion in a window seat invited us to "Sit here on this window cushion to hear the walls whisper." When you sat down, your weight turns on a tape of several people trash talking the Royals. Inaudibly unfortunately.

Chapter 27 – The London Eye Regards Sherlock Holmes and We the Food and Drink

From the announcement plans of the London Eye, through construction and successful establishment of it, Richie has followed the story and frequently expressed his longing to visit it and take a spin. Fearing heights, engineering errors, and a bad moon rising, I had no desire at all to get on it.

So he bought an express ticket that hurled him to the head of the line and I settled down in a nearby restaurant patio to write postcards. Both of us were content until an icy wind off of the Thames drove me into the restaurant.

After Richie floated off of the Eye, wrapped in bliss, we got down to more mundane matters, i.e. lunch.

We walked over the Millennium Bridge to an area near Trafalgar Square where a bar-restaurant called The Sherlock Homes caught our eye. The downstairs is the pub part; upstairs is the more formal restaurant with a mini-museum of Holmes' office, complete with such as his glasses, Watson and a dead black bear. Keeping up the theme, the key to the unisex bathroom was attached to a giant magnifying glass.

Richie ordered the Ploughman's Special (8.95 pounds) and we shared an order of garlic mushrooms in a cream sauce over crispy bread - which wasn't when the sauce settled in – (5.95 pounds.) I ordered a "giant Yorkshire pudding" with beef gravy and could only manage about a third of it. When the Brits say "giant," much like the Texas' emphasis on size, they aren't kidding.

And We Regard Food and Drink in England

Before we ever left for England, a friendly guy at a local store asked, "Do you like hot foods?"

"Yes!" I enthused.

"Well, take a little bottle of Tabasco with you – only a few places have ever heard of it." I laughed at the absurdity of carrying a little bottle of Tabasco around with me.

I rued my laughter when I realized that Burning Hot! to many of the English is (drum roll) malt vinegar.

I could have used a lot of Tabasco in the Bloody Mary served on board BA on the way to London.

At the hotel dining room, I ordered a gin martini. "Of course, mohdam ("madam" in Britspeak.) He brought a clear liquid on the rocks in a small glass. I grinned with anticipation and took a swallow and thought I was hallucinating somehow. It was sweet! He'd used sweet vermouth. He tried again with dry vermouth, but my fervor for gin had faded.

Another day, late afternoon, we went in to a pub not far from the hotel and since it was a crowd of 30-somethings, I thought I'd have better luck.

When I ordered a gin martini, the bartender asked with interest, "What's that?"

I explained and he said, "We don't serve many mixed drinks – just mainly beer and wine," and shrugged. Clearly the customer (me) is not always right and he was letting me know it. I sighed and ordered a gin and tonic. At least he'd heard of gin and tonic water.

In summation, bring the bottle of Tabasco. You might also smuggle in the smallest size vermouth made. They've got plenty of gin!

After touring The Tate, we ankled over to the Albion Pub for a spot of lunch. Richie ordered the Classic Burger (10.20 lbs) and I threw caution to the winds and ordered the BBQ Pulled pork with coleslaw and chips (9 lbs.) When Richie told our waitress "Medium" for his hamburger, she said, "Oh sir, it can only be well-done – health laws," looking wise. She all but jerked her chin and winked. If she'd had "Mad Cow" tattooed across her forehead, it couldn't have been plainer.

I thought my pulled pork would surely come with malt vinegar as "barbecue sauce" but it didn't. It had the real deal.

Of note: pubs are replacing the use of china plates for sandwiches with 2 in. thick wooden planks. They aren't as sanitary as china because germs sink into the wood.

The older the building, the more likely the unisex bathroom will be upstairs. Often up stairs so tight they seem like climbing a giant corkscrew.

Trenchant sign in a pub bathroom: A night you'll never forget! A night you can't remember! Pace yourself!

Speaking of bathroom matters, Tube station toilets are usually 50 pence per use, but the ones at Blackfriar station are free! Make a note.

Euston Station's Ladies room has a couple of "wide cubicles" for the anorexically challenged. So – they DO have fat people in London! We are not alone!

Chapter 28 – London's "Friendly" Bar

Richie named it that. We got off of the Tube at Earls Court, our station, and Richie spotted it across the street. "C'mon, let's have a pint," he said.

It was clearly an old building, but the corner pub was well-kept-up with a crimson-colored pressed tin ceiling and a long, faded red cushion on the banquette that ran along under a side window. Neat little tables with chairs faced the banquette.

Me, not the fat lady, snout deep in a beer. Note ceiling.

The only vacant seats were on the banquette between two men and a really fat lady. We approached and I asked if anyone was sitting there, pointing to the space.

"No, no! Sit yer selves down!" came the genial reply of the two gents. The lady patted the space next to her and gestured welcomingly. Gratefully, I started to sit down, but the space was so narrow due to the lady's bulk that I almost fell into the man's lap. Wedged between them, I sat down and then down some more and finally bottomed out so to speak on the boards supporting the "cushion." I apologized profusely to the man who waved it away, "No worries, luv."

Richie went to the bar for a pair of Stella's and I looked about me. The lady was looking at me with open curiosity.

Of course, she started talking to us. Her accent was "foreign" but I couldn't tell from where. Richie point blank asked her if she was from the Caribbean and she smiled mysteriously.

She said that she was going to be late for an appointment – she'd only been sitting here trying to decide between a cab and the Tube. She said that London's Tube was not very accommodating for the handicapped passenger.

She said that with her great weight, she found stairs terrifying and exhausting. But cheerfully added that she was happy being fat! I told her that she was being a "fat-ist" like being an age-ist and she roared with delight.

She turned to Richie and said that for him, she would make the time to answer his questions. He leaned forward with interest. Since she was nearly sitting on me, I didn't have any trouble hearing her as she launched in to her difficulties learning French! *"A bit off topic,"* I thought to myself.

Again, she told Richie, "You can ask me anything!"

"No, no," we protested sincerely. But she never heard us at all because she launched into learning English, Spanish being her first language. She asked me if I spoke French so I answered in it. She responded in English about how hard English was to learn. Privately I bet myself that she speaks about as much French as our cockatiel.

While I was thinking that, she kept on talking and waving a free hand. The other hand was digging in her purse. She pulled some money out and asked Richie to go to the bar for her and get her two shots of Bell whiskey and a "baby" beer, adding graciously that he could have a drink on her. He declined and went to the bar. Later, he told me that when he ordered her drinks, the bartender looked up and said, "Oh. Her." Clearly, she was no stranger to the place.

Now freshly fueled (she'd dumped the whiskies in the baby beer) she relaxed seemingly forgetting her appointment which was quite possibly a conversational ruse at best. She continued to be as dramatic as a Mexican sunset, waving her hands, making faces and talking incessantly. She complimented me on my beauty (further proof she was loaded) and admired Richie's hair.

Desperate to say something nice back to her, I focused on her make-up which was flawless and I told her so. She gasped in studious surprise and yelled, "That's the exact opposite of some of what my friends say! Thank you! Thank YOU!" and, lurching toward me, began loudly kissing the left side of my face! It was like being caught at Pompeii, but with cascading fat not lava. With every smear of lipstick on my face she said, "SMACK!" I was appalled as you can well imagine and shrieked, "No! No!"

The men on my right thought this was hilariously good fun and very nearly slapped their thighs in glee. Shortly after, they got up to leave, thanked us for the unexpected comedy turn, waved genially and split.

Then a tall, exceedingly thin black man wove into view. He was clearly a happy drunk/drugger who greeted us by saying, "What are three lovely ladies doing in here?" the implication being that our beauty transcended our surroundings.

Richie turned his head and the poor guy hastily backpedaled in alarm. Richie's beard and moustache had come as a shock to the poor guy.

He apologized profusely, but Richie merely nodded. It wasn't the first time and unless he finally gets a normal haircut, it won't be the last either.

The man could have been in his 50s but there was no way to know his age. For sure, this was not his first beer of the day. Nor, possibly, his last joint. If I'd had the proper tools, I could have taken out his appendix then and there, no anesthetic needed.

He was enjoying the music only he could hear and from time to time favored us with a line of song. He volunteered that Bach and Mendelssohn were his favorite composers.

I couldn't resist (it wasn't my first beer of the day either) and said, authoritarily, "And Bobby Darrin..."

"Like, like," he said blissfully and sang another line of something. It was as bizarre an hour as I have ever known. Being enveloped in cascading fat was extremely disconcerting let alone the SMACK business. The fat lady looked ominously near to pouncing again and I knew we had to get out of there.

I looked at my wristwatch, tapped it and said, "Richie, you know we promised to meet the Smythe-Braytons" and he shot me a puzzled look and said, "Who?" I glared. He said, "Yes, yes – let me finish my beer."

He did and we fled to the dubious safety of the street and its rushing traffic, all, of course, driving the wrong way.

The Kings Head up the road was much quieter. For the moment I'd had enough pub joviality for a day.

Chapter 29 – The Dales

"What On Earth Were You Doing There?"

As it happens, the only reason we were in London at all was that dear, but misguided friends who live in Lancashire, had casually invited us to come visit them there!

What they didn't realize until it was far too late is that our motto is "If invited, go!"

Thus, on Day 4, we packed up, and left the hotel, headed for the train that would take us there. Not before some fireworks at the front desk however. Nothing about the bill; paid in full.

But between Richie and myself. It was raining when we were ready to leave. The Tube to Euston Station would require two transfers – during rush hour. It would require me to pull a roll-on suitcase, topped by another bag while clutching my purse (the size of a satchel) under my left arm and then carrying an open umbrella over it all (and me.) I said we'd take a cab instead.

Richie was seriously annoyed that I balked at imitating a camel; he hates spending money on a cab. And we had our Oyster passes and so what was a little rain? I gave him the hairy eyeball of death and turned to the desk and asked them to get a cab.

The desk clerk called their pet cab company, but alas – nothing for 30 minutes. So, the doorman went outside and flagged one down. The cab that stopped was a Black Cab which was another tour goal! To ride in one as the drivers are subjected to an exam called The Knowledge, a series of tests on the location of every street in London. Every lane, half-block street, mews – every bit you can put a car wheel on.

Black Cabs have a different interior than our Yellow Cabs. There is no trunk, for starters. Instead the luggage is piled up against the pull-down seats on the back of the driver's seat.

We had an uneventful ride to Euston Station, albeit in total silence on Richie's part. The driver and I had a lively conversation about The Knowledge (difficult but do-able,) driving in London's biggest peeves (too many to list here)…15 pounds and well worth it.

Euston is a big station with an even bigger patio on one side. This square is dotted with fast-food restaurants, stone benches and people eating or smoking in the rain.

Our train was announced and we hastened to the track. Other than a really, long snout, the Virgin train seemed no different from trains we've ridden in France. The Brits did add a refinement though – a crescent-shaped hard plastic handle on the back of every aisle seat. Presumably to keep one's grubby paws off of the shoulder of the passenger sitting there during a curve. The Brits in my experience are not touchy-feely.

After we got out of London, we saw rolling green fields bordered by rustic-looking (falling down) stone walls. The further north we went the more the rolling hills began to lift themselves into steeper and steeper elevations.

Our hosts met us at Preston station, as arranged, and whisked us off for a quick tour of Haworth, the home of the Bronte family of some literary fame.

When this excursion had been offered, I was privately kind of jealous. I thought, *"I'm a writer, too! And no one cares about my old family home!"* which in retrospect is just as well as it has been a freeway on-ramp for some time now.

Haworth, the home village of these worthies, was first mentioned as a colony in 1209. Today the main industry is tourism and the population in 2011 was a mere 6,379 souls.

The Brontes came to Haworth in 1820 because the *pater familias* was assigned there as the Perpetual Curate of the Church (of England.) The church is conveniently located a short way from the house. They lived in this house for the rest of their lives, as short-lived as some of them proved to be.

By 1822, Mrs. Bronte and two of the older daughters – Marie and Elizabeth – had all died. The only son, Bramwell, became a dissolute drinker and died in 1848 with his family gathered around him. As he had been considered a danger to himself and others prior to his demise, it is likely that some family members weren't all that grief stricken.

Mr. Bronte outlived his wife and all of their children, dying at age 84, something of a record for longevity in those times.

Is the Vet In? Herriot Country

James Herriot, another more successful writer than I am, wrote four books about his experiences as a vet in the Dales. The books are a collection of stories and while the stories are wound around animals, nevertheless, they are a great deal more about the types and personalities of the owners. I have been a fan of his for yonks years and was truly anxious to actually see what I'd only read about. Herriot had a rare descriptive bent.

On the way we passed by the tiny village of Knapely, Yorkshire, where "Calendar Girls" was filmed in 2003 using the women of Knapely.

And Then We Went Out to Dinner We dined at The Craven Heifer Inn, Colne. Villages are rather sparse on the ground in and around the Dales and often you will find a restaurant, bar AND hotel all in the same set of buildings. The Craven Heifer is one of them.

Frank's "Gammon and Egg" interested me greatly. I had no idea what "gammon" was although I think we've all run across mention of it in various books. It looked very like a large ham steak with a fried egg on top.

It turns out that gammon and ham both come from the hind leg of a pig, but: gammon is cured with the bacon and the ham is usually brined.

After some goading on my part, Richie ordered for his dessert the item that intrigued me – an Eton Mess. This is a wild combination of fresh berries, vanilla ice cream, and meringue topped with toffee sauce and Chantilly (whipped) cream.

Chapter 30 – Ta, London – Had a Wonderful Time

And London Said, "Not So Fast, Yank Tourists"

Despite leaving two hours earlier than we'd originally planned on doing to get from "the country" to Heathrow, we missed our flight by five minutes. This after taking three different Tubes from the London train station to get to Heathrow.

Literally. British Air closes the gate at 3:55 p.m. for their last flight of the day to Los Angeles at 4:15 p.m.

Heathrow's Terminal 5 is a confusing tangle of escalators and elevators and the odd dead end. At one point we had to walk over a sheer glass-floored "bridge" high above the 5th floor below us. As I am terrified of heights, this was ... stressful. But it was do it or spend the rest of my life in Terminal 5.

At Bag Check, a mournful-looking man in BA uniform, looked at his watch and sadly said that we'd just missed our flight. He then directed us to the reservations clerk to "re-book" the exact same flight the next day. The fee for rebooking was 275 pounds ($412.50 American.) We could have gone out earlier, but the up-tick in price would have been even more murderously high than the stabbing we' just suffered to Ye Olde Wallet.

To add to our traveling pleasure, British Air had just installed a new computer system and our agent wasn't familiar with it and had to keep calling other agents to come help her out. She finally was able to confirm the change and give us security passes. We'd have to line up the next day to get the boarding passes. More fun!

I went outdoors to a patio for a much-needed cigarette and some personal brood time and Richie went in search of the centralized hotel system desk for Heathrow. My only instruction to him had been to get a smoking-permitted hotel. I didn't care if it was a twin, double or a bag of dirty bedding on the laundry room floor.

Airport Hotel Ransom – Business as Usual

Airport hotels are on to a good thing. For whatever reason, you *have* to spend a night there. They don't care why; they only care that you are there, at their mercy.

The Park Inn Heathrow was no exception. There were three tour buses parked out front and the lobby was filled with people milling about as uniformed tour guides bellowed out names. Corporate types in suits – male and female – crowded the bar. Interestingly, the bar top was luminous glass which cast a really unflattering light up, highlight double chins, nose interiors, etc.

We were given keys and staggered off with our luggage to said room. There were no ash trays in it. I called the desk and was merrily told, "That's because it's a no smoking room!" (elbow dig had I been in the same room.) After some negotiation, we were told to wait there; someone would bring us a key to an okay-to-smoke room.

The new room was a smoking room, but again, no ashtray. I called Housekeeping this time and was politely told that "All of our ash trays are in use right now (HUH?) but I'll check the ballrooms."

In a few moments, there was a tap at the door and an arm handed Richie an ash tray.

We went down to the bar for a necessary pint. Since lunch was only a vague memory; I think we'd shared a small bag of peanuts; we were well ready for dinner. There was a great, long line snaking into the restaurant so we returned to the bar and got a table, an enormous booth that would easily have seated six or eight people.

A nice-looking couple came in, looked at all the filled tables, approached and asked if we would mind sharing the booth?

"Of course not!" we said in unison and they sat down. They were from Norfolk and he was a retired policeman. He said he'd never carried a gun in the entire 30 years of his career. "Only a truncheon," he said with a smile.

They were flying to Chicago the next morning to take a tour of Route 66, all the way to California, where they would fly back to Heathrow.

He told us a funny story. His station got a call from a man the police all knew well. He was threatening to kill himself. When they arrived, he opened the door and stood in the doorway.

In one hand he held a bottle of pills; the other pressed the point of a butcher knife at his heart.

He whined that he didn't know which to use to kill himself and this cop said, "Tell you what, mate – I'll help you out. I'll slam this door!"

We roared. He was an excellent raconteur. Cops usually are and we were lucky to have had the couple's company. She may have heard it before, but she laughed with us.

Chapter 31 – Travelers! Beware Cultural Differences

There's No Tipping in China

Tipping 101, researched and printed by Conde Nast Traveler and ... appropriated by this author.

China has a "no tipping whatsoever" policy in the better hotels which stick you with a 10% extra fee anyhow. But since you can't rid us Americans of the nasty habit of tipping everything that moves, China has relented somewhat – if you insist on tipping, do it quietly and out of sight; never in front of the tipped's boss.

This presents a lovely picture in my mind ... look, I'll show you ...picture a hotel corridor, guest furtively sticks head out of the doorway, spots a maid down the hall – "Pst, pst!" urgently. Maid turns, comes to the doorway (fingering the mace in her apron pocket in case this round-eyes has something funny in mind.) He indicates folding money in his hand; she tightens her grip on the mace. Both look both ways up and down the empty corridor and the man slides the money into the maid's hand. The maid bows silently and scuttles away to count it.

Japan is nearly as secretive . Tips must be enclosed in a clean, white envelope – some department stores even have a money-wrapping department! You should also make the effort to go to the bank and get new bills in *consecutive numbers* if it's at all possible.

Russia used to have a non-tipping policy and people were afraid to accept tips believing that they would be reported to the police for taking bribes! Not any more. Be sure to tip your waiter directly; don't leave the money on the table because management will sidle along and take it! In fact, all of Eastern Europe now expects to be tipped.

In Dubai, Egypt, Israel, Jordan, Brazil, Costa Rica, France and the United Kingdom, the tip is included in your tab – look for the words *"service compris"* on the bill. It's French for "service included" and universally accepted as an explanation for the bill not adding up according to your calculations.

The Flight Attendant Knows Where You're From

"A Frank Steward" is the alias of a former flight attendant on a named-not airline.

He begins his dissertation on Americans because he is one and says that even before we open our mouths, he knows. Americans, according to him, positively exude an air of friendliness.

I had to think about that one for a moment and concluded that he's sort of right. Americans on a foreign carrier to Europe are friendly because they're looking forward to a fun vacation at a dream destination. *Everything* is wonderful to them. They're finally on a plane and *it's gonna happen!*

Not so much within America. New York passengers are sullen and easily pissed off. I have never really understood their habit of applauding when the plane lands. Are they complimenting the pilot or … insulting him. Either way, this unseemly applause for a guy just doing his/her job, doesn't seem to express a lot of confidence in the pilots or airline.

Chicago and DFW tend to be friendlier. In fact, I have never gotten out of DFW without listening to a lengthy answer to any simple question that I might ask one of the natives. Example: (me to a young woman) "Excuse me, do you know what time it is?"

Response: "Oh, hon, no. Mah rat boyfriend got all drunked up and he ripped it right off mah wrist? And stomped on it! Did you evah? Ah told him, 'Ah hope you'ah prepared to buy me another one, you sumvabitch.'"

And DFW offers some of the best people-watching. Where else are you going to see a tall blonde with Big Hair, striding along in denim shorts and cowboy boots? With or without a sequined cowboy hat?

Chapter 32 – Quiero Cabo!

I Want Cabo – Right Now!

Cabo San Lucas is a two hour plane ride from LAX. We have a great hotel, in the heart of town and yet it is quiet and peaceful.

We love Mexican food and you haven't tasted "Fried shrimp" until you've eaten shrimp so fresh they just came off of the boat, were battered, slung into hot fat and brought to you – a maybe 3 ½ minute process.

The scenery is gorgeous – Hotel Row on the corridor from the airport to Cabo has scenic shots all the way to the edge of town. And it's warm enough to stick a bare arm out the car window.

I have business in Cabo. I need to check on the free-range rooster that rules the world in a bar-restaurant – either the Giggling Marlin or the Squid Roe – can't remember. He walks and pecks his way around the tables, hops up on a ceramic bar top and occasionally favors the crowd with raucous crows.

It's worth doing the research, grueling though it may be, to find him. It will require a thorough inspection of both of the above-named bars, lubricated by a Pacifico or two, of course, just to show good manners to the bar owners.

When we find him, we already know not to eat there. And if the rooster's become a broken-down old sot, not to have a beer there either.

I love the glass-bottom boat tours out to Los Arcos, mainly, for the relatively cheap boat ride and the often amusing pilots. We have a favorite in a guy named Chui – enormously fat – who joked that the pelicans were "Mexican turkeys."

When we do this again, I am going to request that we NOT go out into the Pacific side of Los Arcos because it's rougher than a mother-in-law's tongue. I studied the way the plexiglass is inserted into the wooden boat bottom once too often and am still amazed that we didn't have to swim for the calm side. OSHA does not have any counterpart that I ever heard of in Mexico.

Remember that when you are tempted to go parasailing near the beach. We once saw a woman nearly make a face plant on the 6th floor of a hotel in Puerta Vallarta.

I'm hoping that the singing guitar musician will still be at the shrimp place (can't remember the name, know exactly where it is) because he has a beautiful, operatic voice. I asked him if he did indeed sing opera? And he burst into an aria that had the whole place applauding like mad. I started to put money in his container, but he waved it away, saying, "That was my gift to you." Wow!

Fresh shrimp used for French-fried shrimp is heavenly if you come out of the Midwest aka The Land of Frozen French-Fried Shrimp.

Of course, there is nothing wrong at all with grilled or broiled shrimp with a garlic-y or a BBQ sauce finish. Or boiled and served with cocktail sauce and guacamole ... where was I?

The Last Time We Were In Cabo

I went to celebrate my 73rd birthday; Richie and our adopted nephew Rafa went along to see that I didn't celebrate it too much, having witnessed previous occasions when I decided to celebrate something. "It's Guy Fawkes Day!" "Today is National Turtle Day! Let's drink to the noble turtle!"

I was pleased that Rafa wanted to go but his tepid comment was, "I've never been there" which I thought was rather below the mark from what I expected. Such as: "Ah, the chance to explore a new site under your skilled and capable expertise! Oh, the joy!"

He doesn't deserve a commercial after that, but he is good to have along. In addition to being a medical doctor and with a black belt in karate, he is fluent in Spanish. He would be a perfect companion for timid old ladies (with money) who have always wanted to visit a Spanish-speaking country but were afraid. You can book him through me. I'm his agent.

The first bit of drama occurred after we'd arrived at our hotel and were on the sidewalk, headed toward a welcoming cerveza. We saw a pair of couples running like hell down the sidewalk across the street. The gentlemen led by some distance, their women squealing and trying to catch up.

A hotel employee pointed at them and said, "They're trying to get back to their cruise ship before it leaves. If it leaves without them, they're left in Cabo with the clothes they're wearing and whatever cash and credit cards they're carrying. But (he paused dramatically) without their passports – back on the ship – they can't get back in to the U.S." He thought for a moment and added, "Bad situation to be in."

The Giggling Marlin was empty except for us and five or six waiters and two bartenders. We sat down and looked around, sipping our Pacificos. I pointed out the kitchen counter the rooster used to strut across and we all lifted our glasses in silent toast.

For want of anything else to see, I perused the drink menu and found the "Skip and Go Naked" composed of: vodka, gin, brandy, rum, Kahlua, Amaretto, banana liquor and creme de coconut.

If you are able to drink four of them in 30 minutes, the bar will add your name to their Wall of Shame. It was an offer that all of us found easy to turn down. But I really loved the happy-go-lucky name of that drink.

Suddenly, through the door burst a group of maybe 10 young people (hard to tell; they milled around like koi in a pond when the tourists are dropping food) who headed straight to the back of the room to the photo opp.

What was this great photo opp, you wonder? being strung up by your ankles against an oceanic backdrop like the marlin out in front of the bar.

One at a time, participants lay down on a rug on the floor and hold their legs up. Padded ankle binders are clapped on, the attached rope is pulled by a strong man who hoists the person up like a prize marlin. The poser is given a shot of tequila – while hanging upside down – photos! And then is gently returned to the floor. Cell phones flashed as the others took turns and copious pictures and then, as one, they whirled, bounded through the bar to the street and were gone. Only to be replaced 10 minutes later with another group who did the same thing.

It turned out that they were on a scavenger hunt. It was also quite clear that they'd been drinking. I asked Rafa, MD, if a person could still vomit despite being upside down? The good doctor grinned and said, "You can pretty much vomit from any position," ending my curiosity – and any appetite.

The show was over so we returned to the street ourselves, but had to stop at The Jungle which advertised "$1 beers!" Naturally, as we are all rather frugal, we couldn't pass up this God-given chance to save money so we walked in and sat down at the open-air bar and looked around. There were souvenir shops galore. The Tecate cans were icy cold. We decided we should save even more money and called the bartender over.

Later, much later, we tottered back to the Crazy Lobster (breakfast favorite) for $11 lobster dinners and then teetered back down the street to the hotel.

Chapter 33 – Impressions At A Funeral

This particular funeral was held for a woman I'd met only once. Our dear friend Tony's mother succumbed to cancer after having been given hospice care in his home, where we had met her. She was a woman of doughty courage – she greeted us, "Well, hello! I'm not dead yet!" (big laugh.) When her time came, Tony said that she died peacefully, looking forward to seeing her beloved husband and Tony's and six other siblings' Dad.

Viewing at 10 a.m.   Funeral Mass at 1 p.m. Reception 2:30 p.m.

The funeral home wasn't as far as we thought it would be, so there we were at 12 noon. At the Viewing Room door, a lady usher told us that the Rosary had begun, but that we could go inside anyhow. (*Rosary? What Rosary? The program hadn't mentioned any Rosary?*)

The door was thick, the voices inside had been inaudible out in the silent corridor and so the other side of the door was a shock. The room was packed! I haven't seen that many people in one place since the local Dairy Queen gave out full-sized samples back in 1967.

We were forced to huddle just inside the door and due to the press of people, had to either try to climb inside the door frame or disappear into the wall. And still more people came in groups of three, five ...By the time they hit the Third Mystery, I was ready to bail. If you have not said nor heard it, the Rosary could be described as fairly repetitious.

I got my chance to discreetly disappear only a moment later when the door opened yet again and four more people edged their way in. Seizing this opportunity, I went out the door into the lobby. I told the woman at the door that I was giving up my place in favor of family members; saying that we were there only as good friends of the deceased's son.

I sat quietly in the lobby, writing these notes until the usher, who had been listening at a crack in the door, waved urgently to me and hissed, "They're starting the eulogies now!" I came willing, but I was greatly puzzled. The Rosary hadn't been announced and now this sudden segue from the Rosary into listening to the eulogy seemed ... rather abrupt. (Not that I would know.)

My only frame of reference for Catholic funerals were the Masses for my late mother-in-law and later father-in-law. Looking back on those events of 20 years ago, I didn't remember the Rosary being read nor any eulogies from the pulpit or the graveside. *"Must be that they do it differently out here, "* I thought and squeezed back into my allotted 2 sq. in. of space.

The oldest son eulogized their mother and then three of the nieces rose up from the front rows and, to a favorite Hawaiian song, began a dance to celebrate the deceased in the space just in front of the coffin where only her forehead and hairline were visible from our point of view. The nieces were very graceful and moved as one person. It was my first hula at a funeral, but Tony had said that it would be an "island funeral."

With barely a five minute respite, we were ushered into the chapel where pews with heavenly-comfortable long cushions awaited us. The room was considerably bigger than the previous room and everyone spread out accordingly.

The order of the service: welcoming the casket at the top of the aisle by the priest while a soloist sang "Amazing Grace." Then, safely back in his pulpit, the casket parked in front of him, the priest issued a sort of multi-purpose absolution of all present with a general forgiveness thrown in for all present. Then a bit of Scripture followed by a duet.

The priest had a breathy, whispery voice like Jackie Kennedy. He kind of creeped me out at the welcoming of the casket. This breathy little voice was going on about how the coffin coverlet from the altar (and they take it back for the next person at the end of the funeral) is "like a warm blanket for her; she is comfortable now." I didn't think mentioning "warmth" around a dead person was very tactful. Nor that he was doing the grieving members any good by suggesting that she's still alive inside there and needed a blanket.

The next funny thing the priest did was this: during his telling of the Mary and Martha and Jesus story, *he acted out the voices!* Martha was high-pitched; Jesus' was a calming baritone. (And I was dying to laugh.)

He troubled me further on in his Mass of Saints. His insider knowledge was that "everyone you know that has died is with us here and now." (I looked around.)

He then launched into "Jesus is coming to all who are troubled" with great zest and then he gave a sort of General Absolution and moved on to the gifts.

Two family members were sent up the aisle to the back of the chapel, returning with a small, wrapped gift each. The soloist sang "Ave Maria" with the priest kind of moo-ing along with her. At first I couldn't figure out what or who was making that noise, but then the fat lady with the big hat in front of me shifted and I could see that it was him.

Possibly enervated by his moo-through of "Ave Maria" he enthusiastically offered to bless us with the Eucharist – "Even if you haven't made your Confession in some time, just come up here and stand with your hand over your heart to show you love Jesus and I will bless you with the Eucharist!" he shouted, maniacally waving around a communion wafer. Much of the audience surged forth while the soloist sang, "Come Home." I was reminded of a genteel sort of revival.

When the individual blessings got sorted out and the blessed were back in their seats, we rose once again for the coffin's passage back up the aisle, sharp left, out the double doors and into the back of a cream-colored hearse. We were given the option of dropping out then or accompanying the casket to the graveside. I muttered to Richie, "In for a penny; in for a pound," and we strode off to the car in the vast parking lot.

I think every single person there had driven their own car; no ridesharing, because the line following the hearse was so long that a groundskeeper in a golf cart had to come back to lead the rest of the line to the right place.

Once there. I walked in the street for as far as it was possible to do, then grabbed Richie's arm and off we stepped into the lumpy grass with open holes in the ground for vases. I am not used to wearing "heels" (or shoes for that matter; Uggs in winter and boat shoes in summer are both exactly like going barefoot) so it was a treachery-fraught journey for me. To be truthful, I spent that ceremony standing on Oscar Padillo's flat grave market (Thanks, Oscar.)

I looked around with interest and discovered that we had a different priest officiating. Apparently, the facility has Indoor and Outdoor Priests which is rather lavish on their part.

The new or Outdoor priest had a golf course tan and a boyish look, but then I noticed that his hands were those of an old person (and I had only to look down at my own to confirm this.)

His gray hair was cut neatly, with a side part and one little forehead strand cunning combed in the reverse direction of the rest of it. Free tip, guys, for obtaining the boyish look.

At the end of the graveside service, we were invited to stay for the actual placement of the coffin in the hole. I said to Richie, "Let's go watch from the car so I can sit down, these shoes are killing me!" He grinned and said, "Go ahead – in for a penny; in for a pound!" and sauntered off for a good spot from which to see it all.

As I sat, shoes off, toes digging in the carpet, I reviewed all that I had just seen. Indoor Priest had liberally sprinkled the coffin with (presumably) holy water as did Outdoor Priest. Neither one of them though had swung the censor for which I was intensely grateful. I remembered my mother-in-law's service where the priest was so enthusiastic that he nearly gassed out the first three rows of pews. The scent/smoke was so dense that prior to my father-in-law's service, we all begged the funeral director to tell the officiating priest not to be that into it. I'm not kidding – there had been great clouds of incense which took quite awhile to disperse. Every asthmatic in the place was gasping in desperation.

Chapter 35 – Papa Hemingway's Son/Daughter

I think the sad saga of Gregory Hemingway's life and death has been edged discreetly under the carpet. Greg – or Gloria, his preference in later years – was born in 1931 and was the second son of Hemingway's second wife, Pauline. His was said to be a difficult birth and in later years, Papa attributed his son's … less than conventional ways … to it. Papa was born in 1899 which goes far to explain an irrational belief like that.

Greg had been a thorn in poseur macho Papa's side since he was 10 years old and Papa found him in Mama's bedroom, trying on her dresses and stockings. Papa went berserk. Clearly he didn't remembered or didn't count it as the same, but he himself was dressed and coifed as a girl by his own dingbat mother.

When Pauline died suddenly, age 56, Greg blamed Papa and said that Papa killed her. They had been on the phone in a heated argument about Greg, when a hitherto unknown tumor on her adrenalin glad went into overdrive and she died on the operating table. Papa said Greg killed her because he was the source of their argument.

Greg grew up and went on an apparently determined effort to disprove that he was not a little… different. He married four times and sired seven children. His 8th child was adopted.

His paternal duty done, he then unleashed his feminine side and started sex reassignment! He started with breast augmentation, but only had one breast done. The other was left as God made him. Give that a moment to percolate and then learn that he hadn't gotten around yet to fiddling with his genitalia. There's a picture! But I don't want to see it!

Greg was mercurial by temperament and fueled by drugs and alcohol. He presented most often as male, but in Key Biscayne and Cocoanut Grove, nothing was considered outrageous and if "Gloria" came into one of his favorite bars dressed as a woman, friends just shrugged it off. They knew that the next night he might well be Greg again. He was welcomed either way.

The police were less than impressed by either personality as under the influence, Gloria was aggressive and abusive.

His last arrest was for indecent exposure. He was walking stark naked down the middle of the main street at 4 o'clock in the afternoon. He'd paused to pull on a pair of underpants (reportedly a flowered thong) but was carrying his dress and high heels.

The police lodged him in the women's section of Miami-Dade jail and five days later, he was found dead of an apparent heart attack. It was caused, gossips whispered, by his struggles to get into a pair of too-tight pants. He had previously been diagnosed with hypertension and cardiovascular disease.

His older brother Patrick, 88 now, has clearly escaped the Hemingway Suicide Curse (five down so far.) Hemingways offed themselves with such frequency that had they all lived in the same town, remaining relatives could gave gotten a substantial discount from their funeral home of mutual choice.

Hemingway Days, a celebration of his life, held in Key West features a Hemingway look-alike, beard and all, as well as a Pamplona bull run that is considerably tamed down – a bull similar to the buckin' bronco machine in select bars, trundled along on a wheeled platform, tugged by H'way look alikes in white shirts and pants with red bandannas around their neck. Gloria would have wanted a ride.

Chapter 38 - On-going Education - You Really Should Read ...

Driving the Saudis, A Chauffeur's Take of the World's Richest Princesses by Jane Amelia Larson

Larson was a typical wanna-be movie actress and had all of the problems we all know – limited income; big rent. To keep herself and her dream going, she looked for a better paying job than Fries At Mickey Ds.

So she signed up to be a limo driver for a firm that often ferried stars, directors, producers and other hot shots around. Having proved herself capable, she was assigned what she thought would be a primo assignment.

A royal Saudi family was coming to town for seven weeks. The extended family required 40 chauffeur-driven luxury vehicles (with the odd SUV thrown in for the help.) The drivers would be on call 24 hours a day, seven days a week. Each driver had an assigned passenger.

Larson was the only female driver. She was assigned as part of the women's entourage and she noted rather quickly that the Saudi women came to Beverly Hills for two reasons – to shop and to get plastic surgery. One woman got breast implants and, post surgery, found a bra that she loved ($500 per bra) and sent Larson out to buy all that she could find in every color they came in. Larson covered Beverly Hills, Orange County and San Diego and garnered 60 of them; a task she spent all day on, for a grand total of $30,000 – for bras. The princess didn't even thank her, a recurring situation.

Larson came to realize that the Saudis were not in any kind of imminent danger from outsiders, but the drivers and noticeable security guys made them feel important, special.

Saudi rules are stringent. All of the women came off of their 747 discreetly covered from head to toe. But: when they arrived at the various hotels, gone were the robes and veils. They wore short, tight skirts, mile-high heels and, generally, looked like working girls.

Larson worked her derriere off, hoping for one of the legendary tips Saudis are said to hand out – as much as $20,000 cash in $100 bills or an extremely expensive watch or both. She daydreamed about the money, but she was to be disappointed.

To ward off sexist attacks from the men, Larson had said that she was married; her husband had been in an accident so she had to work. She was tipped $1,000. The Saudis reasoned that it was her husband's duty to provide for a wife and it was her duty to stay home.

After all, that's how they did it in Saudi Arabia.

"Almost Famous Women" by Megan Mayhew Bergman

This book includes a brief look at women such as Standard Oil heiress, Joe (Joe) Carstairs on her personally-owned island. I should have stated that she was a cross-dressing, cigar chewing heiress. Marlene Dietrich frequented her island and was a … close personal friend.

Others who were out-shadowed by a more famous relation include Lord Byron's illegitimate daughter Allegra; Oscar Wilde's wild niece Dolly; Edna St. Vincent Millay's sister Norma and James Joyce's troubled daughter Lucia.

But the most interesting have to be Daisy and Violet Hilton, co-joined twins. They were born in Brighton, England, to an unmarried barmaid on February 5, 1908 and died, aged 60, in Charlotte, NC, January 1, 1969.

A woman named Mary Hilton helped to deliver the babies and, as they continued to survive as the only pair of Britain's co-joined twins to survive, she began to see commercial possibilities. So she offered to buy them from the barmaid, who accepted her offer with alacrity.

True to her word, she had them out touring as the United Twins by their third birthday. Home conditions at the Hilton residence were not warming. They were kept as virtual prisoners, forced to learn to tap dance (four legs, four arms) and later to play music instruments, the saxophone and violin.

They did relatively well financially, first in vaudeville and when that died, in burlesque. In 1931, they made changes. Daisy dyed her hair blonde and they quit dressing alike. They were co-joined at the hip and buttock, but did not share any major organs, only their blood.

Despite their forced proximity, they had a series of affairs with various show biz types. One of the women wanted to marry, but the judge wouldn't issue a license; he said it was illegal to issue a marriage license to three people.

They spent their last years in Charlotte, NC, working as grocery store clerks. When they didn't show up for work, the store manager sent someone to the house to check on them.

Both were dead of the Asian flu. The coroner decided that Daisy died first and Violet followed her two to four hours later. How chilling is that? Eck.

"Great Expectations – the Sons and Daughters of Charles Dickens" by Robert Gottlieb

Charles Dickens, 24, married Catherine Hogarth, 20, on April 2, 1836. Nine months later, their first son was born and he would be followed by nine siblings. There were at least two miscarriages as well during a 15 year stretch. Clearly amusements in London during those years were few and far between. "Only one thing for it, Maud!" hearty slap across the poor woman's buttocks.

Catherine's younger sister, Mary, came to help with the children. She didn't last long as a mother's helper; after a night at the theatre, she suffered a fatal heart attack and died the next day. She was 17 years old. Dickens then insisted that when he himself died, he must be buried with her. He wore her ring for the rest of his life to the probable dismay of his wife.

Catherine, one of nine in her own family, was not at a loss for finding more help; she promptly recruited her sister Georgina to take Mary's place.

And then in 1857, disaster struck again. Dickens fell wildly in love with an actress named Ellen Terman. Shortly after they met, she retired from the stage and was subsequently supported by Dickens.

A year later, in 1858, he ruthlessly kicked his wife out of their home, after having given her a nice settlement and a new home. As a sort of final thrust of the blade, he refused to let her take the children.

Dickens made nearly a career of welcoming each new baby with enthusiasm and joy; never hesitated to prefer one child over the others, proclaiming said child, "My favorite." As they grew to adulthood, each child, one by one disappointed him. Oldest son Charley defied him at age 21 and often visited his mother.

He was not shy about expressing his feelings about every one of them in private and in public. As a result, only one of the nine (a son) turned out to be a success. So much for Dickens great expectations.

"Breaking Points: Using History, Maxims and Modern Science to Understand Karate" by RH Gutierrez, MD

This is not a good read for people with anger management or poor impulse control issues. If you have either, move along; nothing to see here.

This is essentially a book on personal self-defense. It will teach you in detail exactly how to disarm and/or seriously damage another person who is threatening your personal safety. Note: it is, however, ineffective when applied to a semi or a bus bearing down on you. Strictly to be used against humans.

It would be a helpful book to read if one is an abused wife or girlfriend; a member of a minority group or an older man or woman. (Note to the latter – a cane makes a helluva good defense weapon and there are classes for cane defense.)

Here are two things that I learned – if someone bigger and stronger grabs you by a wrist, instantly drop to one knee. This throws the assailant off balance and, while you're down there, might as well head butt them in the balls which will really discourage a male attacker.

Dr. Gutierrez is a medical doctor. He taught me that the arch of the collarbone is structurally its weakest point and relatively easy to break. If the collarbone gets broken, the arm below it is useless.

Raise your hands high in the "I surrender!" gesture and then slam your fists down. Dr. Gutierrez advises using an elbow rather than a fist, but I wouldn't want to work that close to an assailant.

Disclaimer: Gutierrez is a long-time personal friend of ours and I did the line edit for him. Which he promptly went back through and changed. I did not write one word of the book, but Amazon seems not to understand that and my name is up there as if I co-wrote it which I most assuredly did not do. This is Rafa's genius.

Chapter 36 – The Statue of Liberty, How to be a Hostage Negotiator and Where to Buy Great Bulletproof Clothing

Happy 150th! Who's Your Plastic Surgeon?

The Statue of Liberty was dedicated 10-28-1886. The robed female figure represents Libertas, the Roman goddess of freedom. The "book" in her left arm represents a "tabula amsata" or table of laws and is inscribed 7-4-1776. The day the Declaration of Independence was signed. There is a broken chain at her feet – I never noticed this detail, have you?

She was created by sculpture Frederic Batholdi and he was inspired by Edouard de Laboulaye, who said that any monument to French-American friendship should be a joint project. A deal was cut: the frogs would pay for and provide the statue; the United States would provide the pedestal and the site for it.

Working ahead of himself, Bartholdi made the head and torch-bearing arm first and then, in a clever PR move, the arm and torch were sent to the Centennial Exposition of 1876 and then to Madison Square Park from 1876 to 1883l.

Meanwhile, Americans were having difficulties raising the money to buy the site (Bedloe's Island) and provide the needed pedestal until publisher Joseph Pulitzer (yeah, that one) started a fund. Over 120,000 donations were received, but sadly, most were for less than a dollar.

Finally, President Grover Cleveland dedicated it and New York held its first ticker tape parade in celebration.

The New York weather – ice storms, hail, gusty winds blowing trash against her soft cheeks made a face lift necessary.

She first went under the plastic surgeon's knife in 1938. Her second lift was done to work on the torch and interior and that work took place from 1984 to 1986.

Closed after 911, she was finally ready for guests in 2004 after work had been done on the pedestal and the statue herself.

No one has been allowed on the balcony around the torch since 1916 for "safety reasons." After all, a lady deserves some privacy, don't you think?

Hostage Negotiator – What Do I Say Now?

Read this. **"Stalling for Time, My Life as an FBI Hostage Negotiator by Gary Noesner   226 pages $26**

Noesner retired from the FBI in 2003. He spent 30 years with the Bureau as an investigator, instructor and, finally, as the first chief of the Crisis Negotiation Unit, Critical Incident Response Group. Today he is a Sr. VP with Control Risks, an international firm.

"Hostage negotiation is about managing yourself and the people around you," Noesner wrote. "A hostage situation is dangers because the person holding the hostage is totally unpredictable.

"The negotiator and the SWAT teams cannot go off half-cocked. The negotiator has to suspend his own emotions to get the crazy person to talk, to tell him what is wanted while the negotiator works to make the nut job feel confident talking to him."

Now this kind of a read is right up my alley. I am totally into making deals, coercing others to do my will and convincing others that what I happen to want is more beneficial than what they think that they want. My truck license plate is "DELMAKR or Dealmaker shortened.

Some things learned from Noesner's book:

Listen. Listen to the person, not the leader of the SWAT team who wants to charge in.

Is the person sputtering mindless gibberish? Why? Drunk? Crazy? Off their meds?

What is the person telling you that he wants? A helicopter out on the lawn to whisk him away? For that flight of fancy, the negotiator would buy time for the person to maybe calm down a little by saying, "I don't have that kind of authority; I have to call my boss on that."

This reference to a boss might well resonate with the hostage who undoubtedly at one time or another has had a boss, too. You want the bad guy to gain confidence in your sincerity. Always use a calm, level voice, never authoritarian tones.

What are tidbits you can offer that you do control? Do they want the power and water turned back on? A sandwich? Demands vary greatly.

But always, always, get a concession from the bad guy before you give him anything. Never give away anything but that which is minor.

If you listen – really listen – you can negotiate very nearly anything from a major purchase down to a later bedtime (or not) for your kid. Go for it! Listen up!

The Drug Lords and Dictators Tailor

Making fashionable garments for the fearful, Miguel Caballero owns a company that makes bullet-proof clothing. Oddly enough, the main offices are in Bogota, Mexico City and Sao Paulo.

These items, made from a stronger, more flexible version of Kevlar include a leather jacket for motorcycling or winter casual wear, a reporter or shooter's vest with all sorts of oddly-placed pockets or a polo shirt. The polo shirt is a bit pricey at $3,475 and comes in navy, red or light blue. A size "Medium" weighs 1.8kg and is "dry clean only."

Custom work: Steven Seagal ordered a bullet-proof *kimono* (there's got to be a story there;) Sean "P Diddy" Combs swaggers around in a white dinner jacket. It is widely believed that President Obama wore one of Caballero's bullet-proof suits to his inauguration. Caballero neither confirmed nor denied this.

Other clients include King Abdullah of Jordan; President Hugo Chavez, Venezuela; President

Uribe, Colombia; and Prince Felipe of Spain. Anyone else see a trend here?

And yet, Caballero swears that he doesn't sell garments to the bad guys, i.e. drug lords or other criminals. Interestingly, before delivery, the customer's name and order number is sewn into the garment in case it's stolen from the new owner. Proof of ownership.

Caballero noted that Catholic priests in drug-infested countries buy a vest to wear under their cassock or – new product alert! – they carry an oversized, bullet-proof Bible to be used as a shield. Thus armed, priests feel safer in offering harsh criticisms of drugs and those who traffic in them.

Bonus sale points: If you are shot within six months of receiving your garment, Caballero will replace it *gratis*. These garments are … one shot items.

Chapter 39 – Pawn Shops, Sharing Space – Don't!

"License to Pawn, Deals, Steals and My Life at the Gold and Silver" by Rick Harrison

Harrison, in addition to recounting his life, gives bits of information all through the book, some of which might interest you, too.

If you've ever wondered why pimps (aka social outreach providers) cover themselves in bling? If they're arrested, their cash is confiscated, but their jewelry is not. One of his stable takes a random sampling to the pawn shop and – viola! Bail money.

He refers to ormolu clocks – all gold, gilt and glitter held together with mercury– "Death Clocks" because the person that made the clock had to be younger than 35. All of the men who had worked with mercury to create the clock were dead by that age. Ormolu clocks start at $15,000. No wonder.

He rails at current gun laws. If you buy a "regular" gun, you have to go through all kinds of paperwork. Conversely, anyone can waltz in to a pawn shop and buy an "antique" gun, pay for it and take it home. Many of the guns are still functional...

Did you know that every single transaction at a pawn shop is reported to the Bureau of Homeland Security and the Las Vegas police department on a daily basis. The pawn shop has a 30-day wait before trying to sell the item because that's how long it takes to make sure the item is not hot.

On the Verb "to Share" ...

My sister flew out of Chicago to Paris for a river
cruise north to the Normandie beaches. Naturally,
I'm thrilled that she gets to make this trip. She and
the girlfriend who talked her into doing it have
been buying clothes for at least a month by now.

She mentioned in passing that because she will be
sharing a cabin with a total stranger it was
necessary to buy $100 worth of new pajamas.
Now, all of my pajama buying is done exclusively
at Target. Given their low prices, $100 would be
10 pairs which means one could just put them in
the trash every morning and have more suitcase
room to bring home souvenirs.

But, as usual, I'm straying from the point here.
Sharing a cabin with a total stranger. This gave
me such a *frisson* of horror that parts of me are still
trembling. I told her that no matter the cost, I
would pay dearly to have my own space.

I added that I needed it for my nightly rituals –
others might not be understanding of the goat
sacrifice, the chicken dance and so on… If that
doesn't scare her about her new roomie, I doubt
she can be scared.

Why my horror, you ask? It all started on a seven-
day cruise of the Mexican Riviera 21 years ago.

We were given assigned seating in the dining room with three other couples.

Instead of being allowed to yank out a chair and start eating like wolves, manners compelled us to make polite conversation.

Conversation is hard to pull off when you have run into these people here and there on the ship all day long.

By the second night as I approached the Table of Death and Dessert with a rictus of a grin on my face, I was thinking, "It's show time!"

One of our fellow diners, a woman from Bakersfield, ordered the exact same thing for dinner every single night. A baked potato with all of the trimmings. No soup nor salad, no meat, just a baked potato. Between bites, sour cream dotting her ample chin, she bragged about their wealth, their house, the pool, the club. She flaunted a very large diamond ring.

But: sinisterly enough on the last morning of the cruise, when it is customary to tip your waiters, they never showed up. Perhaps she had room service bring her a big baked potato for the road? They stiffed those poor waiters, pure and simple.

Hazard of the job. People are weird and cheap all over the world.

Back to my original complaint about sharing. I objected to the forced necessity to make conversation. It really was torture as none of us had anything in common.

But infinitely worse would be having to bunk with someone like the woman from Bakersfield.

Chapter 40 – Winging It and Life in Tokyo and Beyond

"Tune in Tokyo, the Gaijin Diaries" by Tim Anderson

Anderson lived in Raleigh, NC, until he decided to take off for Japan. He got a job with an international teaching bureau and away he went. The back flap says, "an irresistible new gay, left-handed, diabetic travel memoir."

There are hysterically funny scenes in the book. He has a gifted and twisted ability to use words. The things I've read so far are an exploration of why Gaijin men?

Over and over, he writes, he sees guys who couldn't get a date for love nor money in the U.S. swanning down the street with exquisitely beautiful Japanese girls?

A Japanese student of his develops an insane crush on him, attending every one of his classes and gazing worshipfully at him. His best friend, a woman named Rachel, tries to square the girl away by telling her the truth: he's gay! Forget about it!"

The girl argues back, "But he looked at my tits!" Apparently that act signals a desire to marry, mate and have children.

Japan is scary.

Who Knew?

That "Kewpie" brand mayonnaise is wildly popular in Japan? The secret: it's made with cider vinegar instead of distilled vinegar. Chefs add other seasonings, notably for spicy rolls, but they also use it as a dipping sauce for sushi, baked mussels or in creamy salad dressings.

That in Korean restaurants, cold dishes will be on your right, hot dishes to your left and the kimchi lurks in the background?

That in a Korean restaurant it's proper etiquette to cover your mouth or turn your head away from older people at your table when drinking alcohol?

That pico de gallo is sometimes called "Mexican salsa" because it's the red, white and green of the Mexican flag?

That the letters that spell out "tip" once stood for To In Sure Promptness, a reference to having been served in a timely manner. I'm guessing "bribe" never really caught on …

That there's a Turkish proverb that says, "He who has no bread has no authority."

That McDonalds across Egypt serve a "McFalafel"? Same as a falafel here, the difference being that it's served on a hamburger bun, not pita bread.

Chapter 41 – Seduction in France – It Rules!

"La Seduction – How the French Play the Game of Life" by Elaine Sciolino

Sciolino is imminently qualified to write about the French as she is the former Paris Bureau Chief for the NY Times. She was decorated as a Chevalier in the Legion of Honor and lives in Paris.

But I think she erred in basing French behavior on only one facet of several possibilities. Sciolino says that there is only one behavior and that it is seduction.

She says that here in America "seduction" has a sexual connotation (and she doesn't think the French are into that?! Hah!) She goes on to posit that much of the interactions between men and women in France would have better been described as "flirtation." There, one flirts to be liked. Simple as that.

She claims that diplomats use seduction, citing the time Richard Holbrooke, the late American diplomat, convinced Madeleine Albright, Secretary of State, to let him be the Chief Administer of Kosovo, by picking a bouquet of edelweiss and presenting to her. He knew she had grown up in Prague near the mountains where the edelweiss grew.

French politicians try to seduce men and women into voting for them. Giscard d'Estaing was famous, even in his '80s! for trying to seduce the ladies, going so far as to write a novel about "a French Head of State and a British Royal" (supposedly Princess Diana.) Such was his prowess that half of France kind of believed it had happened!

But when Sciolino offered insights on French women, I sat up and paid attention. French women go lightly on the make-up. If they do their eyes, they don't wear lipstick. French women have to decide what they want to highlight that day and which goes better with that day's outfit.

Perfume is to be used so lightly that only the person kissing your cheek can smell it. Your scent is meant to evoke memories of yourself in your signature perfume (Shalimar by Guerlain, for example) in an intimate situation, being kissed "Hello" or "Au revoir."

The great Coco Chanel once remarked, thoughtfully, "A woman without perfume is a woman without a future."

Huh. She didn't live in Southern California where every fifth person screams about their allergies.

Want to Be a Crazy Horse Girl?

In America, the double D bra cup is extolled. In France, it's one's derriere that evokes wistful sighs. Given that, I'm surprised that Kim Kardashian with her grotesque hind end hasn't been made President of France.

Only 38 per cent of French men prefer breasts to butts and a full 50 per cent preferred the derriere and legs above all, so to speak.

Maybe French men still believe that a breast should only be big enough to fill the flat champagne glass. Today, of course, champagne is more widely served in a flute and try stuffing a tit into one of them!

Nudity is in the eye of the beholder it would seem. There is a long-running show in Paris called The Crazy Horse Cabaret Theatre which features performers that are never completely nekkid, but whose bodies are "painted with illusionary stripes of light." One thing the girls never, ever take off is – their shoes!

The Directrice of the joint said, "High heels enhance the leg line. Wearing them you will walk differently, you will act differently." In my case, high heels would enhance my orthopods wallet and for sure I would walk differently in a matching pair of boot casts.

It's not easy to become a Crazy Horse dancer. Requirements: you must be between 5 ft. 6 in. and 5 ft. 8 in. tall with no more than 10 ½ in. between your nipples and a mere 5 in. between the navel and pubis. Absolutely no tattoos or plastic surgery. You will be weighed once a week.

Quite a change from Las Vegas where I once amused myself during a bare-breasted revue number by counting the scars for breast surgeries,

appendectomies and the one poor lady who had
had spinal surgery.

The *Directrice* scornfully said, "In Las Vegas,
everything is lit up and bright. There is absolutely
nothing left to the imagination. It (Vegas) doesn't
speak to your brain. It speaks to a few people's
pants, maybe, but not to their brains. And the
brain – that's where the beauty is." Take THAT,
American dudes.

It's not easy to become a Crazy Horse dancer.
Requirements: you must be between 5 ft. 6 in. and
5 ft. 8 in. tall with no more than 10 ½ in. between
your nipples and a mere 5 in. between the navel
and pubis. Absolutely no tattoos or plastic
surgery. You will be weighed once a week.

Quite a change from Las Vegas where I once
amused myself during a bare-breasted revue
number by counting the scars for breast surgeries,
appendectomies and the one poor lady who had
had spinal surgery.

The *Directrice* scornfully said, "In Las Vegas,
everything is lit up and bright. There is absolutely
nothing left to the imagination. It (Vegas) doesn't
speak to your brain. It speaks to a few people's
pants, maybe, but not to their brains. And the
brain – that's where the beauty is." Take THAT,
American dudes.

Chapter 42 – Butter, Black Pepper and Fix-It's

"Much Depends on Dinner: the Extraordinary History and Mythology, Allure and Obsessions, Perils and Taboos of an Ordinary Meal" by Margaret Visser (Unofficial winner Longest Book Title Probably Ever)

Visser was born in South Africa and went to schools in Zambia, Zimbabwe, France and Canada where she now resides. She writes books on social rituals.

She seems to have made a career out of taking an ordinary thing or place and working the hell out of it.

"Much Depends on Dinner" covers the history, what it's used for and why minutiae of a meal of: corn on the cob, chicken and rice and salad. The butter for the corn on the cob set off something inside her and she goes on for pages. I suffered; you can, too.

She posits that butter could originally have come from travelers in northern climes carrying leather bags of milk. As the poor walked and the rich rode, the milk-filled bag jolted and swayed – a primitive butter churn, if you will. Because butter can only be churned in a cool environment, northern Europeans ate it while southern Europe used olive oi.

It was considered so rich in the Middle Ages that it was banned during Lent. But: by paying the Catholic church a fee, one could indulge. The still-called "Butter Tower" of Rouen Cathedral was built from these bribes.

The color of butter used to be determined by the cow's diet. Pale in winter (no grass) and darker in summer. To get a desirable color, people from the Middle Ages onward tinted it with various things – crushed marigolds, carrot juice, saffron and annatto.

During WW2 the shortage of butter meant lard was sold in a plastic bag with a dime-sized inset of bright yellow food dye. To turn the white lard yellow, it was necessary to knead and knead the "butter" around until it was a uniform yellow. Guess who got to do that at our house?

When the Potato Famine hit Ireland with some gusto, butter (used on the potatoes, porridge and bread) became scarce because the cows were dying of starvation.

It became a mark of Christian charity to offer a guest a bit of butter for their bread. So widespread was this practice that one Neidh O'Mulconry's tombstone labeled him "the head of the in-hospitality of Ireland" because he vowed often and publicly that he'd never give bread and butter to guests. Must have made for a great Memorial Day graveside visit for his descendants.

The Irish, Norse, Finns and Scots all flavored butter with garlic. They crammed it in to a "firkin" which is 1/4th the size of a barrel and yields 56 lbs. of, in this case, butter. These quarter barrels were buried (for refrigeration?) in the family bog and it was customary to plant a tree near-by to mark where it had been left.

In Morocco butter is kneaded with various spices and herbs, then cooked, salted, strained and stored in stoppered jugs. Each family takes pride in their ability to produce a fine-smelling "smen" (butter) and occasionally a guest will be allowed the honor of sniffing it. Otherwise, it is saved for galas such as a wedding.

Butter was plentiful except in the winter and it was eaten by the lower class. The nobility might use a pat in a sauce, but it was considered "peasant food" and shunned by them. For their snobbishness they suffered from vitamin A deficiency and got bladder and kidney stones for their pains. Today, the rich will eat a little fat, but not enough to make them fat. God forbid!

Black Pepper
In today's world with its plethora of black, white, pink peppers. It may surprise to learn that pepper of any kind was once so scarce that it was used as money.

In A.D. 410, a guy called Alaric the Visigoth (catchy, eh?) demanded 1 ½ TONS of pepper as a ransom from Rome.

During the Middle Ages in Europe, peppercorns were counted out, one by one. Can't think they'd have much "pepper" to them after that treatment.

In the 11th century, many towns and villages kept their accounts in pepper. One woolen dress – five peppercorns – and taxes and rents were paid in them.

As always, crime comes into it (sigh.) At the turn of the century (but which one was not disclosed) crooked spice dealers would cut their product with …mouse droppings!

During Prohibition, it was common to pepper your martini. The pepper was believed to drag any impurities of the bathtub-made gin down to the bottom of the glass. I've been told that Russians still add pepper to their vodka – and for the same reason.

Today pepper is used for much less exotic uses than "Darling! What a pretty dress? If I can ask … how many peppercorns?"

Fill the foot of an old pair of knee-highs and hang it in the closet to repel moths.

You can keep vermin off of your property (except for Girl Scout cookie sellers and Jehovah's Witnesses) by laying down a trail of pepper along your boundaries.

In the laundry, add a teaspoon of black pepper to the first suds when you're doing cottons as they stop colors from running. Better idea, only wash in cold water.

Add a dash to vanilla ice cream or buttered popcorn for an exotic flavor.

"I Still Have It – I Just Can't Remember Where I Put It" by Rita Rudner

"I'm an only child, which means I was overprotected. My tricycle had seven wheels. And a driver."

"My last credit card bill was so big that before I opened it, I actually heard a drum roll."

"When you get older, you really appreciate sleep. It's the best of both worlds, you get to be alive and unconscious."

Rudner was born (or so says Wikipedia.com 9/17/1953 so she's not that old.

But I am. The mammogram tech told me to keep my bra on; the machine can't get that close to the floor.

Chapter 43 – Never Fish Under a Bridge; The End Is Nigh

A Few of the 10,001 Things of Dr. Bader. Sounds like an *avant guarde* German film title, doesn't it?

Never fish near a bridge or off of one. The pollution from vehicles is tremendous. That fish which looks so shiny and good can make you sick.

If you lose a contact lens in the evening, turn the lights off and use a flashlight to explore the ground. The lost lens will reflect the light.

Got one of those pressurized lids with the little button thing in the middle – think jar of pickles – and the dot won't pop no matter how hard you try twisting the lid? Take a beer can opener and using the tip upside down, lever gently along the bumped out edges, pulling them out just a little. Pop! It'll open.

Is eating fish really necessary for heart health? Harvard tracked 45,000 men and their eating habits. The heart attack rate for men who ate fish six times a week was the same as it was for men who only ate it twice a month!

River fish are said to have more flavor because they have to swim against the current and thus they exercise more than a lake fish where the water is … largely motionless. One of you alert readers should write a children's book – The Industrious River Fish and the Indolent Lake Fish and What Happened to Them. Send the royalties to: address.

There's a good reason that I love shrimp and that is basically because they aren't fish. True, the cholesterol content of shrimp is higher than that of fish, but the cholesterol count for shrimp is lower than any other type of meat product and doesn't have a lot of saturated fat.

I know people who love their steak rare. It makes me cringe and want to run away when I see the bright red blood pooling on their plate. But, wait! That isn't blood says Dr. Bader. He says it is a pigment called myoglobin (found in all meats) that gives the liquid a reddish color. Blood gets its color from hemoglobin. The red juices are, for the most part, colored by it and water.

Hotdogs were first sold in America at Coney Island, Brooklyn, by a German immigrant named Charles Feltman. Muscling in on his business was one Nathan Handwerker (Nathan's Hot Dogs) began selling them, too. He made his employees wear white coats and stethoscopes to denote cleanliness after a rumor spread that hod dos were made from ground dog meat! Hot dogs aren't made of wiener dogs!

The End Is Nigh ...

Richie had a Major American Airline (MAW) retirees lunch to attend and came home with a folder they'd all received and discussed. It was a folder for end-of-life decisions! This monthly luncheon of late has been specializing in Disasters for the Old and Somewhat Confused. Recent months brought us elder abuse, setting up finances before your mind is gone and now this.

The folder was labeled "Your Way" and is put out by the Healthcare and Elder Law Programs (HELP) Corporation funded largely by the Ahmanson Foundation.

It's a patient's directory which covers what is to be done – or not done as the case may be – if the patient is unable to speak for him/herself. Get your FREE copy today! Help4srs.org.

Talk about detailed! Three sets of papers; a general guideline about how you feel regarding long-term illess, persistent vegetative states and death; full funeral instructions and the legal work to declare another person, not related, as your "helper." I particularly liked a section called "Your Additional Feelings and Views."

1. In making decisions for me, obtain the views of these people – list them.

2. In making decisions for me, ignore the views of these people – list them

The Instructions Concerning My Funeral and Burial

Arrangements are practical and never more so then when someone dies suddenly. Sample: "I desire that the following persons be my pallbearers." Okay... Eric Clapton, George Clooney, Elton John ...

You are asked to list those who are invited to speak (pick people you can trust to say something nice about you "very nearly qualified for sainthood when she (fill in)" or have the chance to speak ripped right out of their showboating hands - "I desire that the following person(s) be notified but ONLY after any service has been held." Hah!

But seriously, all of this should have this kind of … personalized documentation. When you've completed the paper work, put it in a safe place and make copies for those directly involved.

Once you've done this, sit back, relax and prepare to emulate my cousin Robert who said that he is not going to die. He's going to ascend.

Chapter 44 – An Editorial, Selfies Can Make Us Rich and Perfection Anxiety

Truthiness My Foot

The LA Times managed to irritate me before I was halfway through my morning cereal. The front page of the Calendar (show biz) section reads:

A HOST OF QUESTIONS – Will Colbert's *truthiness* survive the "Late Show" switch?

TRUTHINESS What are these people playing at?! I looked it up and discovered that it is a word "invented" by Colbert himself.

I didn't think there would be a definition, but there is and it's this:

Truthiness is a quality assigned to a person claiming an argument is right based on a gut feeling and has nothing to do with logic, evidence or intellectual examination of facts.

Certainly describes politicians, doesn't it?

Making a fortune with Selfies

Selfies used to be called "self-portraits" when the times had a little more dignity than nowadays. But in 2002 the term "selfies" went into effect and became a common (and how) word for a specific activity.

Right after people became obsessed with phoning home photos of themselves in unlikely places so did accidental death rates rise astonishingly for such as the girl who wanted to be just a little farther from the camera so she took a step backward and fell off the cliff/into the shark tank/ under the train wheels – your choice.

Thanks to their devotion to themselves, teenagers and narcissists may just provide a financially secure dotage for me. I'm already in old age. I'm talking about the fact that I may be in for a big, fat royalty fee with my sensational idea.

I'll share it with you, Gentle Readers, because I know that none of you would be low enough to steal it. However: know that if you did, my wrath would be horrific and my ways of revenge are limitless. Ya ready?

Selfie Paper Dolls! Now you can play with yourself endlessly! Don't confine yourself to sending photos. That's so 2002.

Here's how it goes – put on your best (or in some cases cleanest) underwear and pose. Stand up straight, arms outstretched, head up and *smile*! You've just created your very own paper doll!

Now, go through your clothes closet, selecting outfits. Don't forget seasonal changes! When you have a goodly pile of clothes, lay them out on a flat surface in the same position as your underwear shot. Click away, print it all up and use your scissors to cut everything out. Use a business-sized envelope as your very own doll's briefcase! Painting said envelope to resemble a little suitcase is optional.

Tuck the envelope in your purse or backpack and discover the fun you can have with other selfie paper doll creators. You can borrow outfits, trade them and never go near a fitting room! I can see Selfie Parties – think Mary Kay or Avon. It's a money saver at the clothing store, too – you'll never buy a mini-skirt when you should be wearing a maxi!

Perfection Anxiety – the Newest Mental Disorder

The words are self-explanatory, but the meaning is not for the likes of us. It is a term to describe those who have 15 houses, yachts in three oceans (nice touch that,) private 747s, plastic surgery and house accounts with all of the couturiers. Well, you ask, "What's left to yearn for?"

The. Very. Best. Nothing less than utter perfection is allowed in the front door even if the butler says it's okay.

A case in point. Petra, daughter of Bernie Ecclestone, and her husband James Stunt (not making that name up) have purchased Van Dyke's last self portrait (he obligingly died a year after painting it) for $20 million dollars. The National Portrait Gallery, London, is fighting to buy it and keep it in England being as Van Dyke was the first portraitist of the land. (harrumph from the Portrait Gallery.)

They apparently turned to making this purchase after having had a $19 million wedding where the bride swanned around in a $130,000 Vera Wang wedding dress among the guests sipping Chateau Petrus ($6,000/bottle.) Then the delirious couple sauntered together, hand-in-hand, into the sunset.

The article was unclear as to whether their saunter ended at their new house (Aaron Spelling's old one, purchased for $85 million or to Petra's London house in Chelsea (90 million Euros.)

The dilemma now swirling about the unfortunate couple would seem to rotate around the disquieting thought, "How do we top this? Why don't we feel better? I mean (stutters slightly) look at all we've got!"

A great many of us can remember specific financial successes that didn't amount to a great deal of money. I will always remember when I sold my first article and photos for $200! A fortune in those days!

I suppose that "the Christian thing" to do would be to feel sorry for them. But I can't. They've bought their own way into Perfection Anxiety, let'em wallow in it. Somewhere else, preferably, then in the pages of *Vanity Fair* or *The Tatler.*

Chapter 46 – The Dark Side of Astrology

Public astrology, i.e. those that run in newspapers and magazines, are generally flattering "Such-and-such is generous to a fault" or else warnings "The 7th house of the 12th moon is affecting your mojo unfavorably, so (sign) you need to ..."

Not here. And if you've read this far, you never expected gentle treatment from this author anyhow. Let us ...

Aries the Ram 3-21 to 4-20

Will butt heads with anyone from God on down over anything. Pushy, selfish and fearless, they yell until people give them whatever they are demanding, just for some peace.

Belligerent to all and charitable to none, their movements are quick, capable and they are credit card abusers. They will cheerfully pay, but you have to catch them first.

They prefer glory to money but manage to spend abundant amounts anyhow.

They only have friends or enemies and the latter outnumber the former by the millions. Gifted in gab and daubed in bullshit, they can talk for hours on subjects they know nothing about.

They are blind, deaf and dumb to anything that they don't want to know and fail to recognize defeat when it is staring them in the face. They forget the past, have no interest in the future and are only interested in today. Famous Aries include Bette Davis, Nikita Krushcev.

Taurus the Bull 4-21 5-21

Silent and quiet, they simply want to be left alone and given their monumental stubbornness and boring manner, they usually get what they want.

Taurus have large bodies and slow, thick minds. Considered homebodies, they seldom leave their pastures as they are too lazy to go visiting.

Crude and earthy, the Bull enjoys slapstick humor, banana peel falls and are totally unable to understand the more subtle forms of humor.

Cheap as they are, they will stir themselves to seek out a bargain which is about the only time they get any speed up other than from comfortable couch to dining room chair. Taurus enjoys the power of decision-making, but turns the scut work over to subordinates. While others turn wrenches, the Bull sits on his haunches and smokes a cigar.

The Bull does have an additional fault – as if they needed any – but it makes them marginally interesting. The Taurus has an absolutely, raging temper when excited. They are the ones the criminal definition of *"crime passional"* or "murder in the 3rd" were written to describe. Famous Taurus include Harry Truman and Adolf Hitler.

Gemini the Twins 5-22 6-21

Fast as greased lightning, these two-faced escape artists are shifty-eyed with receding hairlines that think fast on their feet. They have to as they are often on the run from the law.

Born with a phone in one hand, they are always early or late, never on time for anything. Gemini have been given the twisted thinking powers of the average politician; they change their minds faster than a prom queen in the back of a '57 Chevy, a person and location the male Gemini loves.

Born blackmailers, the Gemini has a selective memory and is shifty by nature. All Geminis have a nickname and in some cases, a police record. All is not always as it is seen with a Gemini. Famous Gemini include Jack Kennedy (with a girl in every closet) and Donald Trump.

Cancer the Crab 6-22 7-23

Fat, lazy, moody and depressing, the Cancer is such a worrywart that many of them keep canned goods under their beds "just in case." Easily hurt, the Crab will scuttle underneath any nearby object to avoid anger, punishment, or a critical word.

Often bad-tempered because they hate the world, never the less, the Cancer loves the spotlight, but is too tired to try to achieve any fame.

Secretive and possessive, the Cancer native often does not know if it is male or female as this sign's men are just as happy cooking dinner as the females are changing a tire.

Cheap and calculating, the Crab will finally help you out if, after the second time you go under the water, it is clear that no one else is going to help you out (literally) they will.

Cancers have a manic phase, brought on by the full moon. They will act very strangely indeed. Famous Cancers are Phyllis Diller, Nelson and John D. Rockefeller.

Leo the Lion 7-24 8-23

Arrogant and vain, they are lazy extroverts. Born convinced that they are royalty, the Leo roars with rage if you try to tell them to do anything. You are there to do for the Leo! Superior and condescending in manner, they love to tell others how to do everything. The Leo has the gift of delegating unimportant tasks and decision-making on important ones – "You install the engine, I have to decide which driving shoes to buy."

When broke, which they often are due to living and entertaining like kings, the Leo is nevertheless sure that more money is on the horizon.

They love to gossip and are either picky neat or desperate slobs about themselves and their environment.

In the midst of a towering rage, they will stop it instantly to preen themselves and blush over a compliment. Famous Leos include Napoleon Bonaparte and Jacqueline Kennedy Onassis.

Virgo the Virgin 8-24   9-23

Ignored and subsequently lonely because they are so picky and precise, the Virgo, if given the opportunity, will talk the hind leg off of a donkey which is probably the only thing that will stand and listen to their endless carping about others or the state of their health (precarious) at all times with a list of their medicine chest items. They are very uncomfortable in crowds, due to their hypochondriacal belief that a germ is just about to land at any time.

They love to criticize others, but hate being criticized themselves.

Virgos are good for something, however, if you can shut them up. They love doing detail work all by themselves with no assistance. Free to take endless time over nitpicking details, the Virgo happily works on and on and on. Virgo examples are Lyndon Johnson (remember his gall bladder scar display?) and Greta Garbo ("I vant to be alone."

Libra the Scales   9-24   10-23

Naïve, gullible and chatty, the Libra balances being warm, friendly and open with cold, quarrelsome and a closed mind. They love to play peacemaker in an argument and then start the argument all over again by then taking the other side. Alternating periods of intense activity in bars and bordellos, the Libra then collapses and would not move a muscle if his hair was on fire.

Open-minded and fair, Librans love the opposite sex and even their own. In short, they will pursue anything that looks like it might be easy.

Unable to be decisive, their favorite remark is, "On the other hand ..." Famous Librans   Bridgette Bardot and Oscar Wilde.

Scorpio the Scorpion   10-24   11-22

Vicious and scheming, bent only on revenge, the Scorpio is a dangerous adversary. They are usually blank-faced while the mind behind works desperately to get something on you. It is not enough for a Scorpio to win; they have to leave scorched, salted earth behind them.

Tremendously interested in sex and intrigued by the shady side of life, many Scorpios have done time – Charles Manson springs to mind ... Others include Bobby Kennedy and Marie Antoinette.

Sagittarius the Archer   11-23   12-21

Too honest or stupid for their own good, The Sag will say the first thing that pops into his mind.

Happy and gregarious – "Childlike" many say – the Sag has no knowledge of financial matters whatsoever. They are gamblers with bad tempers and will, as they say in Texas, "hitchee" if crossed.

The good news is that they react quickly and will hit you with a fist, but not shoot you.

Unable to keep a secret, they are also unable to tell jokes. Prone to momentary enthusiasms, a Sag will deny loving words fully meant at the time, but instantly forgotten on getting out of bed. Examples are Frank Sinatra and William Buckley, Jr.

Capricorn the Goat   12-22   1-20

Upwardly mobile, the goat will swallow any insult, any slight, to keep rising higher and higher. Power mad and luxury driven, they will bootlick anyone above them.

They marry for money or position and then become even more snobbish.

Weak and sickly as children, surprisingly (and sadly) they live the longest of any of the zodiac signs. They revere anything old, such as: old money, old yachts, or old T-bills. They enjoy being people users behind the scenes. Famous Capricorns are Richard M. Nixon and Martin Luther King, Jr.

Aquarius the Water Bearer   1-21   2-19

Genuinely crazy or just light-hearted, these people are the experimenters in such as bizarre combinations of drugs, alcohol and experimental living arrangements such as the extended harem.

First to try anything new, they find everything interesting. The men look like women and *vice versa,* that's how mixed up this sign is. They are not fussy about their sexual preferences – anything still living.

They have an instinctive ability to get along with patients in mental hospitals. They are airheads, totally unaware of responsibility or duty. An Aquarius would rather give you money than loan it to you. But good luck getting any money out of these cheapskates. Examples Ronald Reagan and Jack Lemmon.

Pisces the Fish   2-20   3-20

Creative and artistic, careless about the future, these people go through life bland and uncaring, just following the flow. Often drunk because they love anything liquid, they have no grasp of reality. It was a Pisces who first said, "Some day, my ship will come in" and he has been dockside ever since.

Often too sensitive to live, they will attempt suicide. They have slow metabolisms, poor eating habits and are accident prone.

They do enjoy sex – anyone, anytime, anywhere. They are born actors and can switch from tears as big as golf balls to smiles as wide as a billboard in a nanosecond. Examples Elizabeth Tylor and Ted Kennedy.

The End